Data Scientist

Data Science in the Real World - Deep Dive into Advanced Topics and Emerging Trends

Donovan Brook

© **Copyright 2023 - All rights reserved.**

The contents of this book may not be reproduced, duplicated or transmitted without direct written permission from the author.

Under no circumstances will any legal responsibility or blame be held against the publisher for any reparation, damages, or monetary loss due to the information herein, either directly or indirectly.

Legal Notice:
This book is copyright protected. This is only for personal use. You cannot amend, dis-tribute, sell, use, quote or paraphrase any part or the content within this book without the consent of the author.

Disclaimer Notice:
Please note the information contained within this document is for educational and entertainment purposes only. Every attempt has been made to provide accurate, up to date and reliable complete information. Readers acknowledge that the author is not engaging in the rendering of legal, financial, medical or professional advice. The content of this book has been derived from various sources. Please consult a licensed professional before attempting any techniques outlined in this book.

By reading this document, the reader agrees that under no circumstances is the author responsible for any losses, direct or indirect, which are incurred as a result of the use of information contained within this document.

Table of Contents

Introduction 5

Chapter One: Deep Learning and Neural Networks ... 9

Chapter Two: Natural Language Processing (NLP) Advances 20

Chapter Three: Graph Analytics and Network Science 31

Chapter Four: Bayesian Methods and Probabilistic Programming 43

Chapter Five: Advanced Reinforcement Learning 58

Chapter Six: Causal Inference and Causal Discovery 72

Chapter Seven: Privacy-Preserving Data Analysis ... 82

Chapter Eight: Time Series Analysis in the Real World 96

Chapter Nine: Advanced Feature Engineering Techniques 106

Chapter Ten: Explainability and Interpretability in Machine Learning 119

Chapter Eleven: Emerging Trends in Data Science . 129

Conclusion 141

Introduction

The chapter on "Recap of Foundational Data Science Knowledge" in the book "Data Scientist: Data Science in the Real World - Deep Dive into Advanced Topics and Emerging Trends" aims to provide readers with a comprehensive review of the essential principles and techniques that form the basis of data science. This recap is crucial in ensuring that readers have a solid understanding of the fundamental concepts required to grasp the advanced topics and emerging trends discussed in the subsequent chapters.

Exploratory Data Analysis (EDA):

Exploratory Data Analysis involves techniques for comprehending data structure and characteristics. It encompasses tasks such as data profiling, data cleaning, handling missing values, outlier detection, and feature scaling. By utilizing popular libraries such as Pandas and NumPy, readers will gain hands-on experience through code examples demonstrating the implementation of these EDA techniques.

Statistical Analysis:

Statistical analysis is integral to drawing meaningful insights and making data-driven decisions. This section provides a review of fundamental statistical concepts, including probability distributions, hypothesis testing, confidence intervals, and regression analysis. Through code examples and mathematical formulas, readers will develop a solid understanding of the practical application of statistical techniques in real-world scenarios.

Machine Learning Algorithms:

Machine learning forms a core component of data science. This recap covers both supervised and unsupervised learning algorithms, encompassing linear regression, logistic regression, decision trees, random forests, k-means clustering, and principal component analysis (PCA). By examining code examples, readers will gain insight into training, evaluating, and fine-tuning machine learning models.

Feature Engineering:

Feature engineering involves transforming raw data into meaningful features that enhance model performance. This section reviews essential techniques such as feature selection, extraction, and transformation. Topics covered include one-hot encoding, feature scaling, feature interaction, and dimensionality reduction using techniques like PCA. Code snippets using libraries like scikit-learn provide practical demonstrations of these techniques.

Model Evaluation and Validation:

Evaluating and validating models is crucial for assessing their performance and generalization capabilities. This recap covers evaluation metrics such as accuracy, precision, recall, F1-score, and Receiver Operating Characteristic (ROC) curves. Techniques for cross-validation, model selection, and performance assessment are discussed, and code examples illustrate the process of model evaluation and validation using functions from scikit-learn.

Data Preprocessing and Transformation:

Before applying machine learning algorithms, data often requires preprocessing and transformation. This section covers techniques such as data cleaning, handling missing values, encoding categorical variables, and scaling numerical features. Imputation, one-hot encoding, label encoding, and standardization methods are explored, and practical code examples demonstrate their implementation using Python libraries.

Data Visualization:

Data visualization plays a crucial role in communicating insights effectively. This recap introduces the principles of effective data visualization and explores popular visualization libraries such as Matplotlib and Seaborn. Different plot types, including scatter plots, bar charts, histograms, and heatmaps, are discussed, along with their appropriate usage in different scenarios. Code examples demonstrate the creation of visualizations to convey data insights.

Conclusion:

The recap of foundational data science knowledge in "Data Scientist: Data Science in the Real World - Deep Dive into Advanced Topics and Emerging Trends" serves as a comprehensive review, ensuring readers have a solid understanding of the fundamental principles and techniques necessary for the advanced topics covered in subsequent chapters. By revisiting these core concepts, readers will be well-equipped to delve into the depths of data science and effectively tackle complex real-world challenges.

Chapter One

Deep Learning and Neural Networks
Neural network architectures (CNN, RNN, GAN)

The field of deep learning has witnessed remarkable advancements in recent years, with neural network architectures playing a central role. This section provides a comprehensive overview of three widely used neural network architectures: Convolutional Neural Networks (CNN), Recurrent Neural Networks (RNN), and Generative Adversarial Networks (GAN). By understanding the principles and applications of these architectures, readers will gain valuable insights into their potential for solving complex real-world problems.

Convolutional Neural Networks (CNN):

Convolutional Neural Networks, or CNNs, have revolutionized the field of computer vision by achieving state-of-the-art results in image classification, object detection, and image segmentation tasks. This architecture's core strength lies in its ability to automatically learn hierarchical representations from image data. CNNs consist of multiple convolutional layers, pooling layers, and fully connected layers. Convolutional layers apply filters to capture local patterns, while pooling layers downsample feature maps to extract relevant information. The fully connected layers integrate the extracted features for classification or regression tasks.

Code Example: A simple example of a CNN architecture implementation using the popular deep learning library TensorFlow:

```
import tensorflow as tf

# Define the CNN architecture
model = tf.keras.Sequential([
    tf.keras.layers.Conv2D(32, (3, 3), activation='relu', input_shape=(32, 32, 3)),
    tf.keras.layers.MaxPooling2D((2, 2)),
    tf.keras.layers.Conv2D(64, (3, 3), activation='relu'),
    tf.keras.layers.MaxPooling2D((2, 2)),
    tf.keras.layers.Flatten(),
    tf.keras.layers.Dense(64, activation='relu'),
    tf.keras.layers.Dense(10, activation='softmax')
])

# Compile and train the model
model.compile(optimizer='adam',
    loss='sparse_categorical_crossentropy',
    metrics=['accuracy'])
model.fit(train_images, train_labels, epochs=10,
    validation_data=(test_images, test_labels))
```

Recurrent Neural Networks (RNN):

Recurrent neural networks (RNNs) are designed to process continuous data, making them well suited for tasks such as natural language processing and speech recognition. RNNs maintain an internal memory state that can capture dependencies between elements in a sequence. A key feature of RNNs is their ability to handle inputs of varying lengths through repetitive connections. However, traditional RNNs suffer from the vanishing gradient problem, which affects their ability to capture long-term dependencies.

Code Example: An example of an RNN architecture implementation using the Keras library:

```python
import tensorflow as tf

# Define the RNN architecture
model = tf.keras.Sequential([
    tf.keras.layers.Embedding(input_dim=vocab_size,
output_dim=embedding_dim,
input_length=max_sequence_length),
    tf.keras.layers.SimpleRNN(128),
    tf.keras.layers.Dense(64, activation='relu'),
    tf.keras.layers.Dense(num_classes,
activation='softmax')
])

# Compile and train the model
model.compile(optimizer='adam',
    loss='sparse_categorical_crossentropy',
    metrics=['accuracy'])
model.fit(train_sequences, train_labels, epochs=10,
validation_data=(test_sequences, test_labels))
```

Generative Adversarial Networks (GAN):

Generative Adversarial Networks (GANs) are a powerful class of generative models that can learn how to generate realistic synthetic data. A GAN consists of two neural networks.

generator network and discriminant network. A generator network learns to produce synthetic data that resembles the real data, and a discriminator network learns to distinguish between real and synthetic data. GANs are iteratively improved through an adversarial training process. The generator tries to fool the discriminator, and the discriminator strives to be able to distinguish between real and fake data more accurately.

Code Example: An example of a GAN architecture implementation using TensorFlow and Keras:

```python
import tensorflow as tf

# Define the generator and discriminator networks
generator = tf.keras.Sequential([...])   # Generator architecture
discriminator = tf.keras.Sequential([...])   # Discriminator architecture

# Compile the discriminator
discriminator.compile(optimizer='adam',
loss=tf.keras.losses.BinaryCrossentropy(from_logits=True))

# Define the GAN architecture
gan = tf.keras.Sequential([generator, discriminator])

# Compile the GAN
gan.compile(optimizer='adam',
loss=tf.keras.losses.BinaryCrossentropy(from_logits=True))

# Train the GAN
gan.fit(train_images, epochs=epochs, batch_size=batch_size)
```

Understanding the architecture and principles behind neural networks is crucial for data scientists working on advanced data science topics. Convolutional Neural Networks (CNNs) are great for computer vision tasks, Recurrent Neural Networks (RNNs) are great for sequential data analysis, and Generative Adversarial Networks (GANs) offer great synthetic data generation capabilities. By understanding these architectures and their implementations, a data scientist can apply his skills to tackle complex real-world challenges and explore the frontiers of emerging data science trends.

Transfer learning and domain adaptation

Transfer learning and domain adaptation are powerful techniques in the field of machine learning that allow models trained on one task or domain to be leveraged for improved performance on related tasks or domains. In this section, we explore the concepts and techniques behind transfer learning and domain adaptation, highlighting their significance in addressing the challenges of limited labeled data and domain shift. Transfer learning:

Transfer learning is a machine learning technique that uses knowledge gained in one task (the source task) to improve the performance of another related task (the target task). Transferring the learned representation allows the model to benefit from pre-trained knowledge and generalize it better to perform tasks in scenarios with limited labeled data. Transfer learning is particularly useful when the source and target tasks share similar characteristics or have related underlying structures.

Code Example: A common approach to transfer learning is to use pre-trained models from popular deep learning frameworks such as TensorFlow and PyTorch. Here's an example using the pre-trained VGG16 model in TensorFlow:

```
import tensorflow as tf
from tensorflow.keras.applications import VGG16

# Load the pre-trained VGG16 model
vgg16 = VGG16(weights='imagenet', include_top=False,
input_shape=(224, 224, 3))

# Freeze the layers in the pre-trained model
for layer in vgg16.layers:
    layer.trainable = False

# Add new layers for the target task
```

```python
model = tf.keras.Sequential([
    vgg16,
    tf.keras.layers.Flatten(),
    tf.keras.layers.Dense(256, activation='relu'),
    tf.keras.layers.Dense(num_classes, activation='softmax')
])

# Compile and train the model
model.compile(optimizer='adam',
    loss='categorical_crossentropy',
    metrics=['accuracy'])
model.fit(train_images, train_labels, epochs=10,
validation_data=(test_images, test_labels))
```

Domain Adaptation:

Domain adaptation addresses the challenge of differences between the source and target domains in machine learning tasks. When the distribution of the data in the target domain differs from that of the source domain, models trained on the source domain may struggle to generalize well. Domain adaptation aims to bridge this gap by adapting the model to the target domain using either supervised or unsupervised approaches.

Code Example: One popular approach to domain adaptation is adversarial domain adaptation, which uses a discriminator network to align the source and target domains. Here's an example using the adversarial adaptation method in PyTorch:

```python
import torch
import torch.nn as nn
import torch.optim as optim
from torch.autograd import Variable

# Define the source and target domain datasets
source_dataset = ...
```

```
target_dataset = ...

# Define the model architecture
model = ...

# Define the discriminator architecture
discriminator = ...

# Define the loss functions
classification_loss = ...
adversarial_loss = ...

# Define the optimizers
model_optimizer = ...
discriminator_optimizer = ...

# Perform domain adaptation training
for epoch in range(num_epochs):
for i, (source_data, target_data) in
enumerate(zip(source_dataset, target_dataset)):
# Train the model on the source data
...

# Train the discriminator on the source and target data
...

# Adapt the model using the adversarial loss
...

# Update the model and discriminator parameters
...

# Evaluate the adapted model on the target domain
...
```

Transfer learning and domain adaptation are valuable techniques that enable models to leverage pre-existing knowledge from one task or domain to improve performance on related tasks or domains. Transfer learning aids in overcoming limited labeled data challenges, while domain adaptation addresses the differences between source and target domains. By understanding and implementing these techniques, data scientists can effectively tackle real-world problems and achieve better generalization performance even in scenarios with limited labeled data or domain shift.

Reinforcement learning and deep Q-networks

Reinforcement learning (RL) is a subfield of machine learning focused on learning optimal decision-making guidelines through interaction with the environment. It has received a great deal of attention for its ability to handle complex problems without the need for explicit oversight. This section describes the concepts of reinforcement learning and explores the application of deep Q networks (DQN), a popular RL algorithm that combines deep neural networks and Q-learning.

Reinforcement Learning:

Reinforcement learning is based on the idea of an agent learning to make sequential decisions in an environment to maximize a notion of cumulative reward. The agent interacts with the environment by taking actions, receiving feedback in the form of rewards, and observing the resulting state transitions. The goal is to learn a policy that maximizes the expected cumulative reward over time.

Q-Learning:

Q-learning is a model-free reinforcement learning algorithm that aims to learn an optimal action-value function, known as the Q-function. The Q-function estimates the expected cumulative reward for taking a specific action in a given state. Through an iterative process of exploration and exploitation, Q-learning updates the Q-function based on the observed rewards and state transitions.

Deep Q-Networks (DQN):

Deep Q-Networks (DQN) is a breakthrough algorithm that combines reinforcement learning with deep neural networks. DQN extends Q-learning by utilizing deep neural networks to approximate the Q-function. The key idea is to use a deep neural network as a function approximator to estimate the Q-values for different state-action pairs.

Code Example: A simplified implementation of a DQN using the PyTorch library:

```python
import torch
import torch.nn as nn
import torch.optim as optim
import torch.nn.functional as F
import numpy as np
from collections import deque

# Define the Deep Q-Network (DQN) architecture
class DQN(nn.Module):
    def __init__(self, input_size, output_size):
        super(DQN, self).__init__()
        self.fc1 = nn.Linear(input_size, 64)
        self.fc2 = nn.Linear(64, 64)
        self.fc3 = nn.Linear(64, output_size)

    def forward(self, x):
        x = F.relu(self.fc1(x))
        x = F.relu(self.fc2(x))
        q_values = self.fc3(x)
        return q_values

# Define the DQN agent
class DQNAgent:
    def __init__(self, state_size, action_size):
        self.state_size = state_size
        self.action_size = action_size
        self.memory = deque(maxlen=10000)
        self.gamma = 0.99  # Discount factor
```

```python
self.epsilon = 1.0  # Exploration rate
self.epsilon_decay = 0.995
self.epsilon_min = 0.01
self.model = DQN(state_size, action_size)
self.optimizer = optim.Adam(self.model.parameters(),
lr=0.001)

def act(self, state):
if np.random.rand() <= self.epsilon:
return np.random.choice(self.action_size)
q_values = self.model(torch.FloatTensor(state))
return torch.argmax(q_values).item()

def replay(self, batch_size):
if len(self.memory) < batch_size:
return
minibatch = np.random.choice(len(self.memory),
batch_size, replace=False)
for idx in minibatch:
state, action, reward, next_state, done =
self.memory[idx]
target = reward
if not done:
    target = reward + self.gamma *
torch.max(self.model(torch.FloatTensor(next_state))).it
em()
q_values = self.model(torch.FloatTensor(state))
q_values[action] = target
loss = F.mse_loss(q_values,
self.model(torch.FloatTensor(state)))
self.optimizer.zero_grad()
loss.backward()
self.optimizer.step()

if self.epsilon > self.epsilon_min:
self.epsilon *= self.epsilon_decay

def remember(self, state, action, reward, next_state,
done):
self.memory.append((state, action, reward, next_state,
done))

# Initialize the DQN agent
state_size = ...
action_size = ...
agent = DQNAgent(state_size, action_size)
```

```
# Training loop
for episode in range(num_episodes):
    state = env.reset()
    for step in range(max_steps):
        action = agent.act(state)
        next_state, reward, done, _ = env.step(action)
        agent.remember(state, action, reward, next_state, done)
        state = next_state
    agent.replay(batch_size)

# Evaluate the trained agent
...
```

Reinforcement learning is a powerful paradigm for learning optimal decision-making policies through interactions with an environment. Deep Q-Networks (DQN) extend traditional Q-learning by incorporating deep neural networks to approximate the Q-function, enabling RL algorithms to handle more complex problems. By implementing and experimenting with DQNs, data scientists can explore and develop innovative solutions for real-world challenges that require sequential decision-making.

Chapter Two

Natural Language Processing (NLP) Advances

Word embeddings and contextual word representations

Word embedding and contextual representation of words are fundamental concepts of natural language processing (NLP). They allow machines to understand and express the meaning of words in a slightly different, more expressive and contextual way. Here we explore the concepts of word embedding and contextual word representations, note their importance in various NLP tasks, and provide examples of their implementation.

Word Embeddings:

Word embeddings are dense vector representations of words that capture the semantic relationships and contextual information of words in a lower-dimensional space. These representations enable machines to understand the meaning and similarities between words based on their distributional properties in a given corpus. Word embeddings have become popular due to their ability to capture fine-grained semantic relationships and support downstream NLP tasks such as text classification, named entity recognition, and sentiment analysis.

Code Example: One popular word embedding technique is Word2Vec, which learns word embeddings by predicting the context of words within a large corpus. Here's an example using the Gensim library to train Word2Vec embeddings:

```python
import gensim
from gensim.models import Word2Vec

# Define a corpus of sentences
corpus = [['I', 'love', 'natural', 'language', 'processing'],
    ['Word', 'embeddings', 'are', 'useful', 'in', 'NLP'],
    ['Machine', 'learning', 'is', 'an', 'exciting', 'field']]

# Train Word2Vec embeddings
model = Word2Vec(corpus, size=100, window=5, min_count=1)

# Get the word vector for a specific word
vector = model.wv['embedding']
```

Contextual Word Representations:

Contextual word representations take into account the surrounding context of a word to generate word representations that are sensitive to the specific context in which the word appears. Unlike static word embeddings, contextual word representations capture the varying meanings of words based on their context within a sentence or document. This contextual information is particularly valuable in tasks that require understanding and disambiguating word meanings in different contexts, such as question-answering, machine translation, and sentiment analysis.

Code Example: One powerful model for generating contextual word representations is the Transformer-based language model, such as BERT (Bidirectional Encoder Representations from Transformers). Here's an example using the Hugging Face Transformers library to encode contextual word representations using BERT:

```python
from transformers import BertModel, BertTokenizer

# Load the pre-trained BERT model and tokenizer
model_name = 'bert-base-uncased'
tokenizer = BertTokenizer.from_pretrained(model_name)
model = BertModel.from_pretrained(model_name)

# Encode a sentence into contextual word representations
sentence = "This is an example sentence."
tokens = tokenizer.encode(sentence, add_special_tokens=True)
input_ids = torch.tensor(tokens).unsqueeze(0)  # Add batch dimension
outputs = model(input_ids)
contextual_embeddings = outputs.last_hidden_state
```

Word embeddings and contextual word representations play a crucial role in natural language processing tasks by enabling machines to understand the meaning and relationships between words. Word embeddings capture semantic relationships based on word co-occurrences, while contextual word representations incorporate the surrounding context to generate representations sensitive to specific contexts. By leveraging these techniques and models like Word2Vec and BERT, data scientists can enhance the performance of various NLP tasks, enabling more accurate and nuanced language understanding.

Transformer models (BERT, GPT)

Transformer models have revolutionized natural language processing (NLP) by significantly improving the performance of various language understanding tasks. In this section, we explore two prominent transformer models: BERT (Bidirectional Encoder Representations from Transformers) and GPT (Generative Pre-trained Transformer). We discuss the architecture, training methodology, and applications of these models, showcasing their impact on the field of NLP.

BERT (Bidirectional Encoder Representations from Transformers):

BERT, introduced by Google AI, is a transformer-based model designed to capture bidirectional contextual information from text. Unlike traditional language models that read text in a left-to-right or right-to-left manner, BERT employs a masked language modeling objective to learn representations that incorporate both left and right context simultaneously. This bidirectional nature allows BERT to capture rich contextual information, resulting in state-of-the-art performance on various NLP tasks.

Architecture:

BERT consists of an encoder stack with multiple layers of self-attention and feed-forward neural networks. The self-attention mechanism allows the model to capture dependencies between words in a sentence, while the feed-forward networks help in learning higher-level representations. BERT uses a transformer architecture, enabling efficient parallel computation and capturing long-range dependencies in the text.

Training Methodology:

BERT is pre-trained on large amounts of unlabeled text data using two main objectives: masked language modeling (MLM) and next sentence prediction (NSP). In MLM, a certain percentage of the input tokens are randomly masked, and the model is trained to predict the original masked tokens. This objective encourages BERT to understand the context and relationships between words. In NSP, BERT predicts whether two sentences appear consecutively in the original document or not, facilitating the learning of sentence-level representations.

Code Example: Utilizing the Hugging Face Transformers library, here's an example of loading a pre-trained BERT model and performing text classification:

```
from transformers import BertTokenizer, BertForSequenceClassification

# Load pre-trained BERT model and tokenizer
model_name = 'bert-base-uncased'
tokenizer = BertTokenizer.from_pretrained(model_name)
model = BertForSequenceClassification.from_pretrained(model_name, num_labels=2)

# Tokenize and encode the input text
text = "This is an example sentence."
encoded_input = tokenizer(text, padding=True, truncation=True, return_tensors='pt')

# Perform text classification
output = model(**encoded_input)
logits = output.logits
```

GPT (Generative Pre-trained Transformer):

GPT, developed by OpenAI, is a generative language model based on the transformer architecture. Unlike BERT, which is trained in a masked language modeling setup, GPT is trained to predict the next word in a sequence, making it a left-to-right autoregressive model. GPT is known for its ability to generate coherent and contextually relevant text, making it suitable for tasks such as text generation, language translation, and dialogue systems.

Architecture:

GPT consists of a stack of transformer decoder layers, where each layer has self-attention and feed-forward neural networks. During training, the model learns to predict the next word given the context of the previous words. This allows GPT to capture the dependencies between words and generate coherent text based on the learned representations.

Training Methodology:

GPT is trained using a language modeling objective, where the model is tasked with predicting the next word in a sequence. Large amounts of unlabeled text data are used for pre-training, allowing GPT to learn a wide range of language patterns and generate contextually appropriate text. Fine-tuning is then performed on specific downstream tasks by training the model on labeled data with task-specific objectives.

Code Example: Using the Transformers library, here's an example of generating text with a pre-trained GPT model:

```
from transformers import GPT2LMHeadModel, GPT2Tokenizer
```

```
# Load pre-trained GPT model and tokenizer
model_name = 'gpt2'
tokenizer = GPT2Tokenizer.from_pretrained(model_name)
model = GPT2LMHeadModel.from_pretrained(model_name)

# Generate text
input_text = "Once upon a time"
input_ids = tokenizer.encode(input_text,
return_tensors='pt')
output = model.generate(input_ids, max_length=100,
num_return_sequences=1)
generated_text = tokenizer.decode(output[0],
skip_special_tokens=True)
```

Transformer models, such as BERT and GPT, have had a profound impact on the field of natural language processing. BERT's bidirectional approach enables it to capture rich contextual information, while GPT's autoregressive nature allows it to generate coherent and contextually relevant text. By leveraging the power of transformers, data scientists can achieve state-of-the-art results on various NLP tasks, including text classification, language generation, and machine translation, thereby advancing the capabilities of language understanding and generation models.

Text generation and dialogue systems

Text generation and dialogue systems are crucial components of natural language processing (NLP) that enable machines to generate coherent and contextually relevant text. These systems have a wide range of applications, including language generation for chatbots, virtual assistants, and automated content creation. In this section, we delve into the concepts and techniques behind text generation and dialogue systems, exploring both rule-based and machine learning approaches.

Rule-Based Approaches:

Rule-based approaches to text generation involve defining explicit rules and patterns to generate text based on specific criteria. These rules can be designed manually or derived from domain-specific knowledge. Rule-based systems excel in generating structured and template-based responses but may lack the ability to generate diverse and creative output.

Code Example: Here's an example of a rule-based text generation system using Python:

```python
import random

# Define a set of templates
templates = [
    "Hello, how can I help you?",
    "What are you looking for today?",
    "Welcome! How may I assist you?"
]

# Generate a response using a random template
response = random.choice(templates)
print(response)
```

Machine Learning Approaches:

Machine learning-based text generation and dialogue systems leverage large amounts of data to learn patterns and generate contextually relevant responses. These systems can be categorized into two main types: retrieval-based and generative models.

Retrieval-Based Models:

Retrieval-based models generate responses by retrieving pre-defined responses from a large collection of predefined utterances or dialogue examples. These models typically use similarity metrics, such as cosine similarity or semantic similarity, to match user input with the most relevant response. Retrieval-based models are computationally efficient and can provide coherent responses, but they are limited to the responses available in their training data.

Code Example: An example of a simple retrieval-based dialogue system using a TF-IDF vectorizer and cosine similarity:

```
from sklearn.feature_extraction.text import TfidfVectorizer
    from sklearn.metrics.pairwise import cosine_similarity

# Define a corpus of predefined responses
corpus = [
    "Hello, how can I assist you today?",
    "What is your preferred payment method?",
    "How can I help you with your order?"
]

# Create a TF-IDF vectorizer and fit it on the corpus
vectorizer = TfidfVectorizer()
X = vectorizer.fit_transform(corpus)

# Compute cosine similarities between user input and predefined responses
user_input = "Can I pay with a credit card?"
user_vector = vectorizer.transform([user_input])
similarities = cosine_similarity(user_vector, X)

# Retrieve the most similar response
most_similar_index = similarities.argmax()
response = corpus[most_similar_index]
print(response)
```

Generative Models:

Generative models, such as recurrent neural networks (RNNs) or transformer-based models like GPT, learn to generate text by modeling the probability distribution of sequences. These models can generate highly creative and contextually relevant responses, but they require substantial amounts of training data and computational resources.

Code Example: Here's an example of using the Hugging Face Transformers library to generate text with a pre-trained GPT-2 model:

```
from transformers import GPT2LMHeadModel, GPT2Tokenizer

# Load pre-trained GPT-2 model and tokenizer
model_name = 'gpt2'
tokenizer = GPT2Tokenizer.from_pretrained(model_name)
model = GPT2LMHeadModel.from_pretrained(model_name)

# Generate text
input_text = "Once upon a time"
input_ids = tokenizer.encode(input_text, return_tensors='pt')
output = model.generate(input_ids, max_length=100, num_return_sequences=1)
generated_text = tokenizer.decode(output[0], skip_special_tokens=True)
print(generated_text)
```

Text generation and dialogue systems play a vital role in various NLP applications, enabling machines to generate coherent and contextually relevant text. Rule-based approaches offer simplicity and control but may lack diversity, while machine learning-based approaches, such as retrieval-based models and generative models, leverage large amounts of data to generate more contextually appropriate responses. By combining these approaches and leveraging advanced machine learning techniques, data scientists can develop sophisticated dialogue systems that mimic human-like conversation and enhance user experiences in various domains.

Chapter Three

Graph Analytics and Network Science
Graph representation and properties

Graphs are basic mathematical constructs used to model the relationships and interactions between objects. In the field of data science, chart visualization and analysis are valuable tools for understanding complex networks, social connections, and interconnected data. This section reviews charting techniques and key properties of charts, along with associated algorithms and code examples.

Diagram display:

A graph consists of vertices (also called nodes) and edges. Vertices represent entities and edges represent relationships or connections between entities. There are several common ways to represent graphs, such as adjacency matrices and adjacency lists.

Adjacency matrix:

An adjacency matrix is a square matrix that represents the connections between vertices. This is usually called a binary matrix, where the rows and columns correspond to the vertices and the value in each cell indicates whether there is an edge between the vertices.

Code Example: Here's an example of representing a graph using an adjacency matrix in Python:

```python
import numpy as np

# Define the number of vertices
num_vertices = 5

# Initialize an empty adjacency matrix
adj_matrix = np.zeros((num_vertices, num_vertices))

# Add edges to the graph
edges = [(0, 1), (1, 2), (2, 3), (3, 4), (4, 0)]
for edge in edges:
    vertex1, vertex2 = edge
    adj_matrix[vertex1][vertex2] = 1
    adj_matrix[vertex2][vertex1] = 1

# Print the adjacency matrix
print(adj_matrix)
```

Adjacency List:

An adjacency list represents a graph as a collection of lists, where each vertex has a list of adjacent vertices. This representation is more space-efficient for sparse graphs compared to the adjacency matrix.

Code Example: Here's an example of representing a graph using an adjacency list in Python:

```python
from collections import defaultdict

# Initialize an empty adjacency list
adj_list = defaultdict(list)

# Add edges to the graph
```

```
edges = [(0, 1), (1, 2), (2, 3), (3, 4), (4, 0)]
for edge in edges:
    vertex1, vertex2 = edge
    adj_list[vertex1].append(vertex2)
    adj_list[vertex2].append(vertex1)

# Print the adjacency list
for vertex, neighbors in adj_list.items():
    print(f"Vertex {vertex}: {neighbors}")
```

Graph Properties:

Graphs possess various properties that help in understanding their structure and behavior. Some important properties include:

1. Degree: The vertex degree is the number of edges connected to the vertex. In directed graphs, degree is further classified into in-degree (number of input edges) and output degree (number of output edges).

2. Path: A path is a series of vertices connected by edges. Path length is the number of edges the path contains.

3. Connectivity: A graph is connected if there is a path between any two vertices. If not, it is disconnected and can be divided into connected components.

4. Cycles: A cycle is a path that starts and ends at the same vertex, passing through different vertices in between. A graph with no cycles is called acyclic.

5. Centrality: Centrality measures the importance of vertices in a chart. Examples of centrality metrics are degree centrality, closeness centrality, and betweenness centrality.

6. Clustering: Clustering measures the tendency of vertices in a graph to form groups or clusters. It provides insights into the presence of communities or densely connected regions in the graph.

Graph algorithms, such as breadth-first search (BFS), depth-first search (DFS), and Dijkstra's algorithm, leverage these properties to perform various graph operations and analyses.

Graph representation and understanding graph properties are fundamental to analyzing complex networks and interconnected data. By utilizing adjacency matrices or adjacency lists, data scientists can efficiently represent graphs in code. Understanding key graph properties, such as degree, connectivity, cycles, centrality, and clustering, allows for insightful analysis and the application of graph algorithms. Incorporating graph analysis into data science workflows provides valuable insights into relational data, social networks, recommendation systems, and other domains that involve interconnectedness.

Centrality and community detection

Centrality and community detection are essential concepts in graph analysis, providing insights into the importance of vertices and the structure of communities within a graph. In this section, we explore centrality measures and community detection algorithms, discussing their significance in understanding graph structures and their applications in various domains.

Centrality Measures:

Centrality measures quantify the importance or influence of vertices within a graph. Different centrality metrics capture distinct aspects of a vertex's significance in the network. Here are some commonly used centrality measures:

1. Degree Centrality:

    Degree centrality measures the number of edges connected to a vertex. Vertices with higher degrees are considered more central as they have more connections.

2. Closeness Centrality:

    Closeness centrality measures how close a vertex is to other vertices in the graph. It quantifies the average shortest path length from a vertex to all other vertices. Vertices with higher closeness centrality are more central as they can reach other vertices more quickly.

3. Betweenness Centrality:

    Betweenness centrality quantifies the extent to which a vertex lies on the shortest paths between pairs of other vertices. Vertices with high betweenness centrality act as bridges or mediators within the graph, connecting different communities or facilitating information flow.

4. Eigenvector Centrality:

    Eigenvector centrality considers both the vertex's direct connections and the centrality of its neighboring vertices. It assigns higher centrality scores to vertices connected to other central vertices, indicating influence in the network.

Community Detection Algorithms:

Community detection algorithms aim to identify groups or communities of densely connected vertices within a graph. These algorithms help reveal the underlying structures, functional modules, or social groups present in the network. Here are some widely used community detection algorithms:

1. Modularity Optimization:

    Modularity optimization is a popular community detection algorithm that maximizes the modularity score of a partition. Modularity measures the density of connections within communities compared to the expected density in a random network. Partitioning the graph to maximize modularity helps identify communities with higher internal connectivity.

Code Example: Here's an example of community detection using the Louvain algorithm in Python using the NetworkX library:

```
import networkx as nx
import community
```

```
# Create a graph
G = nx.karate_club_graph()

# Detect communities using the Louvain algorithm
partition = community.best_partition(G)

# Print the communities
for vertex, community_id in partition.items():
    print(f"Vertex {vertex}: Community {community_id}")
```

2. Girvan-Newman Algorithm:

The Girvan-Newman algorithm iteratively removes edges with the highest betweenness centrality until the graph is divided into communities. This algorithm focuses on the idea that edges connecting different communities have higher betweenness centrality and removing them reveals the underlying community structure.

3. Label Propagation Algorithm:

The Label Propagation algorithm assigns labels to vertices based on the labels of their neighbors and iteratively updates labels until a stable state is reached. Vertices with the same label are considered part of the same community. This algorithm is fast and scalable, making it suitable for large-scale graphs.

Centrality and community detection techniques provide valuable insights into the structure and dynamics of complex networks. By quantifying the importance of vertices using centrality measures and identifying communities through detection algorithms, data scientists can uncover meaningful patterns and characteristics within graph data. These techniques find applications in various domains, including social network analysis, recommendation systems, identification of functional modules in biological networks, and understanding information flow in networks. Incorporating centrality and community detection analysis enhances our understanding of graph structures and aids in making informed decisions in a wide range of real-world scenarios.

Link prediction and graph neural networks

Link prediction is a fundamental task in graph analysis that aims to predict missing or future connections between entities in a network. With the increasing availability of large-scale network data, link prediction techniques play a crucial role in understanding the underlying structure and dynamics of complex networks. In recent years, the advent of graph neural networks (GNNs) has revolutionized link prediction by leveraging node and edge features to capture intricate relationships. In this section, we delve into link prediction methods and the application of graph neural networks in this domain.

Link Prediction Methods:

Link prediction methods utilize various approaches to infer missing or potential connections in a graph. These methods exploit network topology, node attributes, and other relevant information to estimate the likelihood of a link between nodes. Here are some commonly used link prediction techniques:

1. Common Neighbors:
   The common neighbors method predicts links based on the number of shared neighbors between two nodes. It assumes that nodes with more common neighbors are more likely to be connected in the future.

2. Jaccard Coefficient:
   The Jaccard coefficient measures the similarity between two nodes based on the ratio of common neighbors to the total number of neighbors. Higher Jaccard coefficients indicate a higher likelihood of a future link.

3. Adamic/Adar:
   The Adamic/Adar method assigns a higher weight to common neighbors with lower degrees. It captures the idea that connections with rare or specific nodes are more valuable.

4. Preferential Attachment:
   Preferential attachment assumes that the likelihood of a new connection to a node is proportional to its degree. Nodes with higher degrees are more likely to attract new links.

Graph Neural Networks for Link Prediction:

Graph neural networks (GNNs) have emerged as powerful models for link prediction tasks in graph analysis. GNNs leverage node and edge features to learn representations that capture the complex relationships and structural patterns in the graph. These neural networks excel in capturing local and global dependencies, making them effective in link prediction. Here are some key components and techniques used in GNN-based link prediction:

1. Graph Convolutional Networks (GCNs):

Graph Convolutional Networks (GCNs) are a type of GNN that aggregate information from a node's neighborhood to compute node embeddings. GCNs learn node representations by iteratively propagating and updating information across the graph, enabling them to capture complex graph structures.

2. Graph Attention Networks (GATs):
Graph Attention Networks (GATs) introduce attention mechanisms in GNNs, allowing nodes to dynamically weigh the importance of their neighbors during message passing. This attention mechanism enables GATs to focus on the most relevant neighbors for link prediction.

3. GraphSAGE:
GraphSAGE (Graph Sample and Aggregated) is a variant of GNN that leverages node sampling techniques to generate representative node embeddings. By aggregating information from different neighborhood samples, GraphSAGE learns robust node representations that can be used for link prediction.

4. Graph Embedding Techniques:
Graph embedding techniques aim to learn low-dimensional representations of nodes that preserve graph structure and connectivity. Embedding approaches like node2vec and DeepWalk utilize random walks or neighborhood sampling to generate node embeddings, which can be used for link prediction.

Code Example: Here's an example of link prediction using a graph neural network, specifically a GraphSAGE model, in Python using the PyTorch Geometric library:

```python
import torch
import torch.nn as nn
from torch_geometric.nn import SAGEConv

class LinkPredictionGNN(nn.Module):
    def __init__(self, num_nodes, embed_dim):
        super(LinkPredictionGNN, self).__init__()
        self.conv1 = SAGEConv(embed_dim, embed_dim)
        self.conv2 = SAGEConv(embed_dim, embed_dim)
        self.linear = nn.Linear(embed_dim * 2, 1)

    def forward(self, x, edge_index):
        x = self.conv1(x, edge_index)
        x = self.conv2(x, edge_index)
        x = torch.cat((x[edge_index[0]], x[edge_index[1]]), dim=1)
        x = self.linear(x)
        return torch.sigmoid(x)

# Instantiate the model
num_nodes = 100
embed_dim = 64
model = LinkPredictionGNN(num_nodes, embed_dim)

# Define loss function and optimizer
criterion = nn.BCELoss()
optimizer = torch.optim.Adam(model.parameters(), lr=0.01)

# Training loop
for epoch in range(num_epochs):
    # Forward pass
    output = model(data.x, data.edge_index)
    loss = criterion(output[train_mask], data.y[train_mask])

    # Backward pass and optimization
    optimizer.zero_grad()
    loss.backward()
    optimizer.step()
```

```
# Evaluation
with torch.no_grad():
    predicted_links = output > 0.5
    accuracy = (predicted_links == data.y).sum().item() / len(data.y)

# Print metrics
print(f"Epoch: {epoch+1}, Loss: {loss.item()}, Accuracy: {accuracy}")
```

Link prediction is a crucial task in graph analysis, enabling us to infer missing or potential connections in a network. Traditional methods, such as common neighbors and preferential attachment, provide valuable insights. However, the rise of graph neural networks (GNNs) has significantly advanced link prediction by incorporating node and edge features and leveraging the power of deep learning. GNN models like GCNs, GATs, and GraphSAGE capture complex graph structures, enabling accurate predictions of missing links. By combining GNNs with graph embedding techniques, we can further enhance link prediction performance. These techniques find applications in various domains, including social network analysis, recommender systems, and network-based biology. By utilizing GNNs for link prediction, data scientists can gain deeper insights into the connectivity patterns of complex networks and make informed decisions based on predicted links.

Chapter Four

Bayesian Methods and Probabilistic Programming
Bayesian inference and probabilistic models

Bayesian inference is a powerful framework for reasoning under uncertainty, making predictions, and learning from data. It provides a systematic approach to update beliefs about unknown quantities based on prior knowledge and observed evidence. In this section, we explore the principles of Bayesian inference and the application of probabilistic models in data science.

Bayesian Inference:

Bayesian inference is based on Bayes' theorem, which mathematically describes how prior beliefs should be updated given observed data. It involves the following steps:

1. Prior Distribution:

The prior distribution represents our beliefs about the unknown quantity before observing any data. It encapsulates any existing knowledge, assumptions, or subjective beliefs. The prior distribution is often chosen based on domain expertise or previous data.

2. Likelihood Function:

The likelihood function captures the probability of observing the data given different values of the unknown quantity. It represents the relationship between the observed data and the unknown parameters in the model. The likelihood function is typically derived from a probabilistic model that describes the data generation process.

3. Posterior Distribution:

The posterior distribution is the updated distribution of the unknown quantity after incorporating the observed data. It is calculated by multiplying the prior distribution and the likelihood function and normalizing the result. The posterior distribution provides a probabilistic summary of our knowledge about the unknown parameters after considering the observed data.

4. Bayesian Updating:

Bayesian inference involves iteratively updating the posterior distribution as new data becomes available. This iterative process allows for continual learning and refinement of beliefs. The posterior distribution obtained at one stage serves as the prior distribution for the next stage, incorporating new evidence and updating our understanding.

Probabilistic Models:

We use probabilistic models for Bayesian inference because they provide a formal basis for determining relationships between the data we observe and unknown parameters. These models take into account the uncertainty inherent in these data.

And models give us a flexible representation of complex real-world phenomena. Here are some probabilistic models that are often used:

1. Gaussian (Normal) Distribution:

The Gaussian distribution is widely used because of its simplicity and applicability to many real world problems. It can be characterized by mean and variance, which represent the central trend and distribute the data accordingly.

2. Bayesian Networks:

Bayesian networks are graphical models that represent the probabilistic relationships between variables using directed acyclic graphs. They facilitate efficient probabilistic reasoning by capturing dependencies among variables and allowing for inference and learning.

3. Hidden Markov Models (HMMs):

Hidden Markov Models are probabilistic models used to model sequential data. These consist of hidden states that are not directly observable and observable states that are affected by the hidden states. HMMs have applications in speech recognition, natural language processing, and bioinformatics.

4. Probabilistic Graphical Models (PGMs):

Probabilistic Graphical Models provide a unified framework for modeling complex relationships in data. PGMs combine probability theory and graph theory to represent dependencies between variables in a structured and interpretable manner. Examples include Bayesian networks, Markov random fields, and factor graphs.

Code Example: Here's an example of Bayesian inference using a simple Gaussian model in Python:

```python
import numpy as np
import scipy.stats as stats

# Generate synthetic data
np.random.seed(42)
true_mean = 5
true_std = 2
data = np.random.normal(true_mean, true_std, size=100)

# Define prior distribution
prior_mean = 0
prior_std = 10

# Update the prior with observed data
posterior_mean = (prior_mean * (prior_std ** 2) + np.mean(data) * (true_std ** 2)) / (prior_std ** 2 + true_std ** 2)
posterior_std = np.sqrt((prior_std ** 2 * true_std ** 2) / (prior_std ** 2 + true_std ** 2))

# Compute posterior predictive distribution
posterior_predictive = stats.norm(posterior_mean, posterior_std)

# Make predictions using the posterior predictive distribution
new_data = np.random.normal(posterior_mean, posterior_std, size=10)

# Print results
print("Prior Distribution: Mean =", prior_mean, ", Standard Deviation =", prior_std)
print("Posterior Distribution: Mean =", posterior_mean, ", Standard Deviation =", posterior_std)
print("Posterior Predictive Distribution: Mean =", posterior_predictive.mean(), ", Standard Deviation =",
```

```
posterior_predictive.std())
print("New Data Predictions:", new_data)
```

Bayesian inference and probabilistic models provide a powerful framework for thinking under uncertainty and making data-driven decisions. Bayesian inference enables continuous learning and belief updating by combining prior knowledge and observational data. Probabilistic models such as Gaussians, Bayesian networks, HMMs, and PGMs formally represent uncertainty and allow us to model complex real-world phenomena. Incorporating Bayesian inference and probabilistic models into data science practices improves our understanding of uncertainty and supports more robust decision-making processes.

Markov Chain Monte Carlo (MCMC) methods

Markov Chain Monte Carlo (MCMC) methods are a class of algorithms used to approximate complex probability distributions and perform statistical inference. These methods are especially useful when direct sampling from the target distribution is not currently available, or when the distribution is multivariate. In this part, I intend to tell you about the principles of MCMC methods and their application in data science.

MCMC Sampling:

MCMC methods employ a Markov chain to generate a sequence of samples that approximates the target distribution. The key idea is to construct a Markov chain with a stationary distribution equal to the desired target distribution. By simulating the Markov chain for a sufficiently long time, the samples generated will converge to the target distribution.

The Metropolis-Hastings Algorithm:

The Metropolis-Hastings algorithm is a widely used MCMC method that allows sampling from a target distribution even when it is not directly accessible. It consists of the following steps:

1. Initialization:

   Start with an initial state in the sample space.

2. Proposal Distribution:

   Generate a proposal state from a proposal distribution. The proposal distribution determines the next candidate state based on the current state of the Markov chain.

3. Acceptance:

   Calculate an acceptance probability based on the ratio of the target distribution's values at the proposed state and the current state. Accept the proposed state with this acceptance probability; otherwise, stay at the current state.

4. Repeat:

   Repeat steps 2 and 3 for a predetermined number of iterations or until convergence is achieved.

5. Convergence:

Assess the convergence of the Markov chain by examining diagnostic measures such as the autocorrelation, trace plots, and the Gelman-Rubin statistic.

Code Example: Here's an example of implementing the Metropolis-Hastings algorithm for sampling from a univariate normal distribution using Python:

```python
import numpy as np
import scipy.stats as stats

def metropolis_hastings(target_dist, proposal_dist, num_samples, initial_state):
    samples = [initial_state]
    current_state = initial_state

    for _ in range(num_samples):
        proposed_state = proposal_dist.rvs(size=1)
        acceptance_prob = min(1,
            target_dist.pdf(proposed_state) /
            target_dist.pdf(current_state))
        acceptance = np.random.uniform() < acceptance_prob

        if acceptance:
            current_state = proposed_state

        samples.append(current_state)

    return np.array(samples)

# Define target distribution (univariate normal)
target_dist = stats.norm(loc=5, scale=2)

# Define proposal distribution (univariate normal)
proposal_dist = stats.norm(loc=0, scale=1)

# Set parameters
num_samples = 10000
initial_state = 0

# Generate samples using Metropolis-Hastings algorithm
samples = metropolis_hastings(target_dist,
```

```
proposal_dist, num_samples, initial_state)

# Compute statistics of the samples
sample_mean = np.mean(samples)
sample_std = np.std(samples)

# Print results
print("Sample Mean:", sample_mean)
print("Sample Standard Deviation:", sample_std)
```

Applications of MCMC Methods:

MCMC methods have a wide range of applications in data science, including:

1. Bayesian Inference:

    MCMC methods enable Bayesian inference by approximating the posterior distribution of model parameters. By sampling from the posterior distribution, one can estimate credible intervals, perform hypothesis testing, and make predictions based on Bayesian models.

2. Statistical Modeling:

    MCMC methods are used to fit complex statistical models that involve latent variables, hierarchical structures, or nonstandard likelihood functions. Examples include hierarchical Bayesian models, hidden Markov models, and Gaussian process regression.

3. Machine Learning:

    MCMC methods can be applied to machine learning tasks such as clustering, dimensionality reduction, and generative models. They are especially useful for performing inference on probabilistic graphical models such as Bayesian networks and Markov random fields.

4. Optimization:

   The MCMC method can be used as a stochastic optimization technique to explore the model parameter space and find global or local optimizations of a given objective function.

Markov Chain Monte Carlo (MCMC) methods provide a powerful framework for sampling from complex probability distributions and performing statistical inference. By constructing a Markov chain with a stationary distribution equal to the target distribution, MCMC methods enable the generation of samples that approximate the desired distribution. The Metropolis-Hastings algorithm is a fundamental MCMC method that allows sampling from a target distribution even when direct sampling is not feasible. MCMC methods find applications in Bayesian inference, statistical modeling, machine learning, and optimization, providing valuable tools for addressing real-world data science challenges.

Probabilistic programming frameworks (Stan, PyMC3)

Probabilistic programming is a powerful paradigm that allows data scientists to specify and solve probabilistic models using high-level programming languages. These frameworks enable the flexible creation and analysis of complex models, incorporating uncertainty and making probabilistic inference more accessible. In this section, we explore two popular probabilistic programming frameworks, Stan and PyMC3, and discuss their features, capabilities, and applications in data science.

Stan:

Stan is a probabilistic programming language designed for building and fitting Bayesian statistical models. It provides a powerful and expressive modeling language and an efficient inference engine for sampling from posterior distributions. Stan supports a wide range of models, from simple linear regression to complex hierarchical models.

Features and Capabilities:

1. Flexible Modeling Language:

    Stan uses its own modeling language that is similar to the BUGS (Bayesian inference Using Gibbs Sampling) language. It allows users to specify probabilistic models using a concise and intuitive syntax, including support for priors, likelihoods, and hierarchical structures.

2. Efficient Sampling:

    Stan utilizes a specialized form of Markov Chain Monte Carlo (MCMC) called Hamiltonian Monte Carlo (HMC), which improves sampling efficiency for high-dimensional models. HMC exploits gradient information to propose samples that are more likely to be accepted, leading to faster convergence.

3. Automatic Differentiation:

   Stan automatically computes gradients of the log probability function, which is crucial for performing efficient sampling using HMC. This feature saves users from the burden of deriving and implementing gradients manually.

4. Extensive Probabilistic Functions:

   Stan provides a rich set of built-in probabilistic functions for common statistical distributions, allowing users to easily specify priors and likelihoods. It also supports user-defined functions, providing flexibility to model custom distributions.

Code Example: Here's an example of fitting a simple linear regression model using Stan in Python:

```
import pystan

# Define the Stan model
stan_code = """
data {
    int<lower=0> N;             // Number of data points
    vector[N] x;                // Predictor variable
    vector[N] y;                // Response variable
}
parameters {
    real alpha;                 // Intercept
    real beta;                  // Slope
    real<lower=0> sigma;        // Error standard deviation
}
model {
    y ~ normal(alpha + beta * x, sigma);   // Likelihood
}
"""
```

```python
# Compile the Stan model
stan_model = pystan.StanModel(model_code=stan_code)

# Prepare the data
data = {'N': len(x), 'x': x, 'y': y}

# Fit the model
fit = stan_model.sampling(data=data)

# Print the summary of the posterior distribution
print(fit)
```

PyMC3:

PyMC3 is a Python library for probabilistic programming with a focus on simplicity and extensibility. It provides a high-level interface for specifying and fitting Bayesian models, offering a wide range of probability distributions and advanced inference algorithms.

Traits and Skills:

1. Intuitive model specs:

PyMC3 uses a flexible and intuitive syntax that allows users to specify models in a natural and concise way. It supports a wide range of probability distributions, priorities, and probabilities, making it suitable for modeling many types of data.

2. Automatic Inference:

PyMC3 approximates posterior distributions using advanced inference algorithms such as Hamiltonian Monte Carlo (HMC) and Variational Inference (VI). The best algorithm is automatically selected based on model characteristics.

3. Model checks and diagnostics:

PyMC3 provides a variety of model checking and diagnostic tools, including convergence diagnostics, posterior prediction checks, and visualization capabilities. These features allow users to assess the quality of derived models and identify potential problems.

4. Extensibility:

PyMC3 is highly extensible, allowing users to define custom probability distributions and design custom inference algorithms. It also seamlessly integrates with other scientific libraries in the Python ecosystem to facilitate data pre-processing, visualization and post-processing.

Code Example: Here's an example of fitting a simple linear regression model using PyMC3:

```python
import pymc3 as pm
import numpy as np

# Define the model
with pm.Model() as model:
    alpha = pm.Normal('alpha', mu=0, sd=10)
    beta = pm.Normal('beta', mu=0, sd=10)
    sigma = pm.HalfNormal('sigma', sd=1)

    mu = alpha + beta * x
    y_obs = pm.Normal('y_obs', mu=mu, sd=sigma, observed=y)

# Perform sampling
trace = pm.sample(1000, tune=1000)
```

```
# Print the summary of the posterior distribution
print(pm.summary(trace))
```

Applications:

Both Stan and PyMC3 have wide-ranging applications in various domains of data science, including:

1. Bayesian Data Analysis:

    Probabilistic programming frameworks are particularly well-suited for Bayesian data analysis tasks. They enable modeling complex relationships, incorporating prior knowledge, and performing posterior inference to make probabilistic statements about the data.

2. Machine Learning:

    Probabilistic programming allows you to develop probabilistic models that integrate uncertainty into machine learning tasks. These include Bayesian neural networks, Gaussian processes, and probabilistic graphical models.

3. Decision Making under Uncertainty:

    Probabilistic programming facilitates decision making in situations with uncertain outcomes. It allows the incorporation of prior beliefs, modeling of dependencies, and computation of expected values or optimal decisions.

Probabilistic programming frameworks, such as Stan and PyMC3, provide powerful tools for building and fitting Bayesian models. These frameworks offer expressive modeling languages, efficient sampling algorithms, and diagnostics for assessing model quality. Stan focuses on efficient sampling using Hamiltonian Monte Carlo (HMC), while PyMC3 emphasizes simplicity and extensibility. Both frameworks have a wide range of applications in data science, enabling probabilistic inference, Bayesian data analysis, and decision making under uncertainty.

Chapter Five

Advanced Reinforcement Learning
Policy gradient methods

Policy gradient methods are a class of reinforcement learning algorithms that directly optimize the policy of an agent to maximize its expected cumulative reward. Unlike value-based methods that estimate the value function and then derive the policy, policy gradient methods work by directly updating the policy parameters in the direction of higher expected return. This approach makes them suitable for solving complex problems with large action spaces and continuous action domains.

Introduction:

Policy gradient methods have gained significant attention in the field of reinforcement learning due to their ability to handle high-dimensional and continuous action spaces. They offer a principled way to optimize policies directly, allowing agents to learn in environments where actions are not discrete or can be chosen from a large set of possibilities. In this section, we will explore the key concepts and techniques behind policy gradient methods.

Policy Optimization:

In reinforcement learning, the policy defines the behavior of an agent. It is a mapping from states to actions, representing the strategy the agent employs to interact with the environment. The goal of policy gradient methods is to find the policy that maximizes the expected cumulative reward over time.

The policy is typically represented by a parametric function, such as a neural network, that takes the state as input and outputs the action probabilities or directly the action values. The parameters of the policy function are updated through gradient ascent to improve the expected return.

Policy Gradient Theorem:

The fundamental result that underlies policy gradient methods is the policy gradient theorem. It provides a way to compute the gradient of the expected return with respect to the policy parameters. The gradient is used to update the policy in the direction of increasing expected return.

The policy gradient theorem can be expressed as follows:

$$\nabla J(\theta) = E[R(t) \nabla \log \pi(a|s; \theta)],$$

where $\nabla J(\theta)$ is the gradient of the expected return J with respect to the policy parameter θ, $R(t)$ is the cumulative reward at time t, $\pi(a|s; \theta)$ is the policy function parameterized by θ, and $\nabla \log \pi(a|s;\theta)$ is the slope of the logarithm of the guideline with respect to θ.

Gradient Estimation:

Estimating the gradient of the expected return is a crucial step in policy gradient methods. One common approach is to use the Monte Carlo method, where the gradient is estimated based on sampled trajectories. By collecting multiple trajectories and computing their returns, the gradient can be approximated.

REINFORCE Algorithm:

The REINFORCE algorithm is a popular policy gradient method that uses the Monte Carlo estimation of the policy gradient. It follows the following steps:

1. Collect Trajectories:

    The agent interacts with the environment, collecting a set of trajectories by following the current policy.

2. Compute Returns:

    For each trajectory, the returns are computed by summing the discounted rewards from each time step. The returns represent the expected cumulative reward for that trajectory.

3. Update Policy:

    The policy parameters are updated using gradient ascent, where the gradient is estimated based on the sampled trajectories and returns. The update step scales the gradient by the learning rate and applies it to the policy parameters.

Code Example: Here's an example of implementing the REINFORCE algorithm using PyTorch:

```python
import torch
import torch.nn as nn
import torch.optim as optim

class Policy(nn.Module):
    def __init__(self, input_size, output_size):
        super(Policy, self).__init__()
        self.fc = nn.Linear(input_size, output_size)

    def forward(self, x):
        x = torch.relu(self.fc(x))
        return torch.softmax(x, dim=-1)

# Create the policy network
policy = Policy(input_size, output_size)
optimizer = optim.Adam(policy.parameters(), lr=0.01)

def reinforce_update(policy, optimizer, trajectories, returns):
    optimizer.zero_grad()

    for trajectory, R in zip(trajectories, returns):
        for t in range(len(trajectory)):
            state, action = trajectory[t]
            log_prob = torch.log(policy(state))[action]
            loss = -log_prob * R
            loss.backward()

    optimizer.step()

# Run the REINFORCE algorithm
for episode in range(num_episodes):
    trajectories = []
    returns = []

    # Collect trajectories and compute returns
    for t in range(max_steps):
        state = env.get_state()
        action = policy(state)
        next_state, reward, done = env.step(action)

        trajectories.append((state, action))
        returns.append(reward)
```

```
if done:
    break

# Update the policy
reinforce_update(policy, optimizer, trajectories, returns)
```

Policy gradient methods provide a powerful framework for solving reinforcement learning problems with continuous action spaces. By directly optimizing the policy, these methods enable agents to learn complex strategies in high-dimensional environments. The policy gradient theorem and algorithms like REINFORCE provide a solid foundation for updating policies based on sampled trajectories and returns. With the advancements in deep learning and the availability of powerful computational tools, policy gradient methods have become increasingly popular and have achieved impressive results in various domains, including robotics, game playing, and natural language processing.

Actor-Critic algorithms

Actor-Critic algorithms are a class of reinforcement learning methods that combine the benefits of both value-based and policy-based approaches. They leverage the strengths of value estimation and policy optimization by maintaining two separate components: an actor that learns the policy and a critic that estimates the value function. This combination allows for more stable and efficient learning in complex environments.

In reinforcement learning, the goal is to find an optimal policy that maximizes the expected cumulative reward. Value-based methods estimate the value function to determine the quality of different actions or states, while policy-based methods directly optimize the policy to maximize the expected return. Actor-Critic algorithms bridge the gap between these two approaches by maintaining separate actor and critic components.

Actor:

The actor is responsible for learning and improving the policy. It receives observations from the environment and outputs actions based on the current policy. The actor can be represented by various models, such as neural networks, that map observations to action probabilities or directly output actions. The actor is updated through policy gradient methods, such as the REINFORCE algorithm or the Proximal Policy Optimization (PPO) algorithm.

Critic:

The critic estimates the value function, which quantifies the expected return from a given state or state-action pair. It helps the actor in evaluating the quality of actions or states and provides feedback for policy updates. The critic can be represented by value-based methods like the Q-learning algorithm or by using function approximation techniques such as deep neural networks. The critic's parameters are updated using techniques like temporal difference learning or Monte Carlo estimation.

Advantages of Actor-Critic Algorithms:

1. Stability: Actor-Critic algorithms offer more stability compared to pure policy-based methods by utilizing value estimation. The critic provides a more reliable

assessment of the quality of actions or states, leading to more stable policy updates.

2. Efficiency: The combination of value estimation and policy optimization enables more efficient learning. The critic's estimates guide the actor towards more rewarding actions or states, reducing the need for extensive exploration.

3. Sample Efficiency: Actor-Critic algorithms can achieve better sample efficiency by reusing experiences. The critic's value estimates can be used as baselines to reduce the variance in the policy gradient updates.

Code Example: Here's an example of an actor-critic algorithm using the Advantage Actor-Critic (A2C) method in TensorFlow:

```python
import tensorflow as tf
from tensorflow.keras.layers import Dense
from tensorflow.keras.optimizers import Adam

# Define the actor network
class Actor(tf.keras.Model):
    def __init__(self, num_actions):
        super(Actor, self).__init__()
        self.dense1 = Dense(64, activation='relu')
        self.dense2 = Dense(num_actions, activation='softmax')

    def call(self, inputs):
        x = self.dense1(inputs)
        x = self.dense2(x)
        return x

# Define the critic network
class Critic(tf.keras.Model):
```

```python
def __init__(self):
    super(Critic, self).__init__()
    self.dense1 = Dense(64, activation='relu')
    self.dense2 = Dense(1)

def call(self, inputs):
    x = self.dense1(inputs)
    x = self.dense2(x)
    return x

# Create the actor and critic models
actor = Actor(num_actions)
critic = Critic()

# Define the optimizer
actor_optimizer = Adam(learning_rate=0.001)
critic_optimizer = Adam(learning_rate=0.001)

# Perform the actor-critic updates
for episode in range(num_episodes):
    with tf.GradientTape() as tape:
        states = []
        actions = []
        rewards = []

        state = env.reset()
        done = False

        while not done:
            states.append(state)

            # Get action probabilities from the actor
            action_probs = actor(tf.expand_dims(state, axis=0))
            action = tf.random.categorical(action_probs, 1)[0, 0]

            # Take the action in the environment
            next_state, reward, done, _ = env.step(action.numpy())

            actions.append(action)
            rewards.append(reward)

            state = next_state

        # Compute the discounted returns
        returns = []
        G = 0
```

```python
for reward in reversed(rewards):
    G = reward + gamma * G
    returns.insert(0, G)

# Convert lists to tensors
states = tf.convert_to_tensor(states)
actions = tf.convert_to_tensor(actions, dtype=tf.int32)
returns = tf.convert_to_tensor(returns, dtype=tf.float32)

# Compute the advantages
values = critic(states)
advantages = returns - tf.squeeze(values)

# Actor loss
action_probs = actor(states)
log_probs = tf.math.log(tf.reduce_sum(action_probs * tf.one_hot(actions, num_actions), axis=1))
actor_loss = -tf.reduce_mean(log_probs * advantages)

# Critic loss
critic_loss = tf.reduce_mean(tf.square(returns - tf.squeeze(values)))

# Update the actor and critic
actor_gradients = tape.gradient(actor_loss, actor.trainable_variables)
critic_gradients = tape.gradient(critic_loss, critic.trainable_variables)

actor_optimizer.apply_gradients(zip(actor_gradients, actor.trainable_variables))
critic_optimizer.apply_gradients(zip(critic_gradients, critic.trainable_variables))
```

Actor-Critic algorithms combine the benefits of value-based and policy-based approaches in reinforcement learning. By maintaining separate actor and critic components, these algorithms offer stability, efficiency, and sample efficiency. The actor learns the policy, while the critic estimates the value function, allowing for more reliable action selection and improved learning in complex environments. The example provided demonstrates the A2C algorithm using TensorFlow, showcasing how the actor and critic components work together to update the policy and value estimates.

Model-based reinforcement learning

Model-based reinforcement learning is an approach to solving reinforcement learning problems by explicitly learning a model of the environment dynamics. Instead of solely relying on interactions with the real environment, model-based methods build an internal representation of the environment and use it to simulate possible outcomes and plan future actions. By leveraging the learned model, these methods aim to improve sample efficiency, enhance exploration, and make more informed decisions.

In reinforcement learning, the agent interacts with an environment, receives observations, takes actions, and receives rewards. Traditional model-free methods, such as Q-learning and policy gradients, learn directly from these interactions. However, model-based reinforcement learning takes a different approach by learning an internal model of the environment's dynamics.

The Internal Model:

The internal model of the environment captures the transition dynamics, which describe how the environment state evolves when the agent takes actions. It typically takes the form of a function or a neural network that predicts the next state given the current state and action. The internal model can also include a reward model to estimate the expected rewards associated with different state-action pairs.

Planning and Decision Making:

With an internal model in place, model-based methods can perform planning and decision-making by simulating possible trajectories and evaluating their expected outcomes. The agent can use planning algorithms, such as Monte Carlo Tree Search (MCTS) or model-predictive control (MPC), to explore different action sequences and estimate their expected returns. By evaluating hypothetical trajectories before executing them in the real environment, the agent can make more informed decisions.

Advantages of Model-Based Reinforcement Learning:

1. Sample Efficiency: Model-based methods can achieve higher sample efficiency compared to model-free approaches. By using the learned internal model, the agent can generate simulated experiences and learn from them without interacting with the real environment. This can significantly reduce the number of interactions needed to learn an optimal policy.

2. Exploration: The internal model allows the agent to explore different action sequences and their potential outcomes in a simulated environment. This exploration can help discover more diverse and rewarding trajectories, leading to better policy learning.

3. Planning and Prediction: With an internal model, the agent can plan ahead and make predictions about the

consequences of its actions. This capability enables more strategic decision-making, taking into account long-term effects and potential risks.

Code Example: Here's an example of a simple model-based reinforcement learning algorithm using a neural network as the internal model:

```python
import numpy as np
import torch
import torch.nn as nn
import torch.optim as optim

# Define the internal model (neural network)
class InternalModel(nn.Module):
    def __init__(self, input_dim, output_dim):
        super(InternalModel, self).__init__()
        self.fc1 = nn.Linear(input_dim, 64)
        self.fc2 = nn.Linear(64, 64)
        self.fc3 = nn.Linear(64, output_dim)

    def forward(self, state, action):
        x = torch.cat([state, action], dim=1)
        x = torch.relu(self.fc1(x))
        x = torch.relu(self.fc2(x))
        next_state = self.fc3(x)
        return next_state

# Create the internal model
input_dim = 4  # Dimension of the state
output_dim = 4  # Dimension of the next state
model = InternalModel(input_dim + output_dim, output_dim)

# Define the planning algorithm (e.g., Monte Carlo Tree Search)
def plan_action_sequence(initial_state):
    action_sequence = []
    state = initial_state
```

```python
for t in range(max_horizon):
    # Generate a set of random actions
    actions = np.random.uniform(low=-1.0, high=1.0,
    size=(num_actions,))
    actions = torch.tensor(actions,
    dtype=torch.float32).unsqueeze(0)

    # Use the internal model to predict the next state
    next_state = model(state, actions)

    # Evaluate the next state's value and choose the best
    action
    values = value_function(next_state)
    best_action = actions[torch.argmax(values)]

    action_sequence.append(best_action.item())
    state = model(state, best_action.unsqueeze(0))

return action_sequence

# Main training loop
for episode in range(num_episodes):
    # Sample an initial state from the environment
    initial_state = env.reset()

    # Plan an action sequence using the internal model
    action_sequence = plan_action_sequence(initial_state)

    # Execute the planned action sequence in the real
    environment
    total_reward = 0
    state = initial_state

    for action in action_sequence:
        next_state, reward, done, _ = env.step(action)
        total_reward += reward
        state = next_state

        if done:
            break

    # Update the internal model using the real interaction
    data
    optimizer.zero_grad()
    loss = compute_loss(initial_state, action_sequence,
    total_reward)
```

```
loss.backward()
optimizer.step()
```

Model-based reinforcement learning offers a promising avenue for improving the sample efficiency and decision-making capabilities of reinforcement learning agents. By learning an internal model of the environment dynamics, agents can simulate possible trajectories and plan actions accordingly. This approach opens up opportunities for more efficient exploration, strategic decision-making, and better overall performance in complex and uncertain environments. The provided code example demonstrates a simple model-based algorithm using a neural network as the internal model, highlighting the steps of planning and executing action sequences based on the learned model.

Chapter Six

Causal Inference and Causal Discovery
Counterfactual reasoning and causal effects

Counterfactual thinking and causal effects are essential concepts in the field of data science, especially causal inference. Understanding and quantifying causality allows us to make informed decisions, understand the impact of interventions, and uncover underlying mechanisms behind observed data. . This section examines the principle of counterfactual thinking and its relationship to causation.

Counterfactual thinking is thinking about what our world would be like if it were different. This gives you the ability to compare results for different hypothetical scenarios and understand the cause and effect relationships between variables here. The basic idea is to contrast observed outcomes with potential outcomes that might have occurred under different conditions.

To illustrate counterfactual considerations, consider a study investigating the efficacy of a new drug for a particular disease. Two groups are observed.

A treatment group receiving drugs and a control group receiving no drugs. An interesting result is an improvement in symptoms. You can define counterfactual outcomes for each individual.

What are the possible consequences of treatment and what are the possible consequences of not treating. But it is impossible to observe both results at the same time in each person, isn't it. This we know as the fundamental problem of causal inference. In return, we rely on statistical methods and assumptions, thus being able to infer causality based on observed or experimental data.

A commonly used method in counterfactual thinking is propensity score matching. The trend value is the probability of receiving treatment considering the observed covariates. By matching people in the treatment group to similar people in the control group based on propensity scores, we can create comparable groups and estimate the causal effect of treatment.

Here's an example code snippet demonstrating propensity score matching using the Python package causalinference:

```python
import numpy as np
from causalinference import CausalModel

# Generate random data
np.random.seed(0)
n = 1000
treatment = np.random.choice([0, 1], size=n)
covariates = np.random.normal(size=(n, 3))
outcome = 5 + 2 * treatment + covariates.sum(axis=1) + np.random.normal(size=n)

# Create a CausalModel object
cm = CausalModel(treatment=treatment, outcome=outcome, covariates=covariates)

# Estimate the propensity scores
cm.est_propensity()

# Perform propensity score matching
cm.match()
```

```
# Estimate the average treatment effect
ate = cm.est_via_matching()

print("Average Treatment Effect:", ate)
```

In this code, we generate random data where treatment represents the treatment assignment, covariates are the observed covariates, and outcome is the observed outcome. We create a CausalModel object and estimate the propensity scores using the est_propensity() method. Then, we perform propensity score matching with the match() method and estimate the average treatment effect using the est_via_matching() method.

Counterfactual reasoning and causal effects go beyond simple association and correlation. They allow us to delve into the causal relationships between variables and understand the impact of interventions. By carefully considering counterfactual scenarios and employing appropriate statistical methods, we can gain valuable insights into the causal mechanisms underlying observed data.

It is worth noting that counterfactual reasoning and causal effects are complex topics with various methods and considerations. This overview provides a glimpse into their significance and introduces one approach for estimating causal effects. To fully grasp the intricacies of counterfactual reasoning and causal inference, further study and exploration of advanced techniques are encouraged.

Causal inference methods (propensity score matching, instrumental variables)

Causal inference methods, such as propensity score matching and instrumental variables, play a crucial role in data science when trying to establish causal relationships between variables. These methods help address the challenges of confounding factors and selection bias, enabling researchers to make more reliable causal claims based on observational or experimental data. In this section, we will explore propensity score matching and instrumental variables as two commonly used approaches in causal inference.

Propensity score matching is a method used to estimate causal effects in observational studies where treatment assignment is not randomized. The propensity score is the conditional probability of receiving the treatment given a set of observed covariates. By matching individuals with similar propensity scores between the treatment and control groups, we can create balanced comparison groups and reduce the impact of confounding variables.

Here's an example code snippet using the Python package causalinference to perform propensity score matching:

```python
import numpy as np
from causalinference import CausalModel

# Generate random data
np.random.seed(0)
n = 1000
treatment = np.random.choice([0, 1], size=n)
covariates = np.random.normal(size=(n, 3))
outcome = 5 + 2 * treatment + covariates.sum(axis=1) + np.random.normal(size=n)
```

```python
# Create a CausalModel object
cm = CausalModel(treatment=treatment, outcome=outcome, covariates=covariates)

# Estimate the propensity scores
cm.est_propensity()

# Perform propensity score matching
cm.match()

# Estimate the average treatment effect
ate = cm.est_via_matching()
print("Average Treatment Effect:", ate)
```

In this code, we first generate random data where treatment represents the treatment assignment, covariates are the observed covariates, and outcome is the observed outcome. We create a CausalModel object and estimate the propensity scores using the est_propensity() method. Then, we perform propensity score matching with the match() method and estimate the average treatment effect using the est_via_matching() method.

Instrumental variables (IV) are another approach in causal inference, especially when dealing with endogeneity or omitted variable bias. An instrumental variable is a variable that is correlated with the treatment assignment but not directly associated with the outcome, except through its influence on the treatment. It serves as a natural randomizer that mimics a randomized controlled trial, helping to identify causal effects.

Here's an example code snippet to demonstrate instrumental variable estimation using the Python package statsmodels:

```python
import numpy as np
import statsmodels.api as sm

# Generate random data
np.random.seed(0)
n = 1000
treatment = np.random.choice([0, 1], size=n)
instrument = np.random.normal(size=n)
covariates = np.random.normal(size=(n, 3))
outcome = 5 + 2 * treatment + 3 * instrument + covariates.sum(axis=1) + np.random.normal(size=n)

# Create a design matrix
X = np.column_stack((treatment, instrument, covariates))

# Perform instrumental variable estimation
iv_model = sm.OLS(endog=outcome, exog=X)
iv_results = iv_model.fit()

print(iv_results.summary())
```

In this code, we generate random data where treatment represents the treatment assignment, instrument is the instrumental variable, covariates are the observed covariates, and outcome is the observed outcome. We create a design matrix X that includes the treatment, instrument, and covariates. Then, we perform instrumental variable estimation using the ordinary least squares (OLS) method with the sm.OLS() function from the statsmodels package.

The code provides summary statistics of the instrumental variable estimation, including coefficient estimates, standard errors, t-values, and p-values. These results help assess the significance and direction of the causal effects estimated through the instrumental variable approach.

Propensity score matching and instrumental variables are powerful tools for causal inference, helping researchers overcome the challenges of confounders and selection bias. By accounting for potential bias and mimicking randomized experiments, these methods provide a more reliable basis for drawing causal inferences from observational data. However, it is important to use them appropriately and interpret results with caution, given the underlying assumptions and limitations of each method.

Discovering causal relationships from observational data

Discovering causality from observational data is a fundamental challenge in data science and causal inference. In many real-world scenarios, it is neither feasible nor ethical to conduct randomized controlled experiments to determine causality. Therefore, researchers often rely on observational data to gain insight into causality. In this section, we consider various approaches and methods for determining causality from observational data.

1. Association and Correlation Analysis:

    One of the initial steps in exploring causal relationships is to analyze associations and correlations between variables. Correlation can provide initial insight and guide further research, although it does not imply causation. Techniques such as scatterplots, correlation coefficients (such as Pearson's correlation), and hypothesis testing (such as t-tests) come to the rescue. They help assess the strength and significance of relationships between variables.

2. Directed Acyclic Graphs (DAGs):

   DAGs are graphical representations used to model causal relationships between variables. They consist of nodes representing variables and directed edges indicating causal connections. By constructing a DAG based on prior knowledge or domain expertise, researchers can visualize and formalize their assumptions about causal relationships. DAGs also provide a framework for identifying confounding variables and potential pathways of causation.

3. Causal Discovery Algorithms:

   Causal discovery algorithms aim to infer causal relationships from observational data without relying on prior knowledge or assumptions. These algorithms employ statistical and computational techniques to identify patterns and dependencies in the data that may indicate causal relationships. Examples of causal discovery algorithms include PC algorithm, GES algorithm, and constraint-based methods like the Causal Bayesian Network approach.

4. Mediation and Moderation Analysis:

   Methods of mediation analysis and mitigation analysis are used to study the mechanisms by which causation occurs. Mediation analysis examines whether the effect of an independent variable on a dependent variable is mediated by one or more intermediate variables. Relaxation analysis, on the other hand, examines the conditions under which causal relationships between variables change. Techniques such as structural equation modeling (SEM) and path analysis can be used for mediation and relaxation analysis.

5. Instrumental Variables and Regression Discontinuity Design:

   Instrumental variables and regression discontinuity design are specialized techniques used when studying causal relationships with specific characteristics. Instrumental variables help address endogeneity and confounding by identifying variables that are independent of the outcome but affect the treatment assignment. Regression discontinuity design focuses on situations where treatment assignment is determined by a threshold or cutoff point, allowing researchers to estimate causal effects near the cutoff point.

6. Propensity Score Methods:

   Propensity score methods, such as propensity score matching and propensity score weighting, are widely used in observational studies to mitigate the effects of confounding variables. The propensity score represents the probability of receiving a treatment given observed covariates. By matching or weighting individuals with similar propensity scores, researchers can create balanced comparison groups and reduce the impact of confounding variables.

When working with observational data, it is crucial to acknowledge the limitations and assumptions underlying the analysis. Causal inference from observational data relies on the assumption of no unobserved confounding, which can be challenging to guarantee. Additionally, the presence of selection bias and measurement error should be carefully addressed to ensure the validity of the causal conclusions.

Overall, discovering causal relationships from observational data requires a combination of statistical analysis techniques, domain knowledge, and careful consideration of the underlying assumptions. By leveraging these approaches, researchers can gain valuable insights into causal relationships, even in the absence of randomized controlled experiments.

Chapter Seven

Privacy-Preserving Data Analysis
Differential privacy and its applications

Differential privacy is a crucial concept in data privacy and protection that has gained significant attention in the field of data science. It provides a rigorous mathematical framework for quantifying and preserving privacy when analyzing sensitive data. In this section, we will explore differential privacy and its applications in data science.

1. Understanding Differential Privacy:

    Differential privacy aims to protect individuals' privacy while allowing for the analysis and utilization of their data. It provides a formal privacy guarantee by ensuring that the outcome of an analysis remains nearly the same, regardless of whether any specific individual's data is included or excluded from the dataset. This prevents any meaningful or sensitive information about an individual from being inferred based on the analysis results.

2. The Epsilon Parameter:

    Differential privacy is defined by a parameter called epsilon (ε), which quantifies the level of privacy protection. A smaller value of epsilon indicates stronger privacy guarantees. A fundamental concept in differential privacy is that adding or removing an individual's data should not significantly change the overall analysis outcome.

3. Privacy-Preserving Data Analysis Techniques:

   Various techniques can be employed to achieve differential privacy in data analysis:

- Noise Addition: One common approach is to add carefully calibrated random noise to the analysis results to protect privacy. For example, adding Laplace noise to numerical data or injecting noise into queries on a database can help preserve privacy while maintaining data utility.

- Data Perturbation: Another technique involves perturbing the original dataset by modifying or transforming certain attributes to prevent re-identification of individuals. This can include techniques such as data swapping, data anonymization, or generalization.

- Query Restriction: Differential privacy can also be achieved by limiting the types of queries or analyses that can be performed on the dataset. By defining a set of pre-approved queries, privacy risks can be controlled and managed effectively.

4. Differential Privacy in Machine Learning:

Differential privacy has significant implications in machine learning, where models often require access to sensitive data for training. Privacy-preserving machine learning algorithms ensure that individual data points cannot be directly extracted or linked to the model's predictions.

- Private Aggregation of Teacher Ensembles (PATE): PATE is a technique that allows for privacy-preserving model training. It involves training multiple "teacher" models on disjoint subsets of the data and then aggregating their predictions using differential privacy techniques.

- Federated Learning: Federated learning enables training machine learning models across multiple decentralized devices or servers without transferring raw data. Differential privacy can be incorporated into federated learning to protect the privacy of individual data contributors.

5. Privacy-Preserving Data Release:

    Differential privacy is also applicable in scenarios where data needs to be released to external parties while preserving privacy. By applying differential privacy mechanisms to released datasets, organizations can share aggregated or sanitized data that is statistically useful but does not compromise individual privacy.

- Synthetic Data Generation: One approach involves generating synthetic data that mimics the statistical properties of the original dataset while preserving privacy. This synthetic data can be released for analysis without revealing sensitive information.

- Secure Multi-Party Computation: Secure multi-party computation techniques allow multiple parties to jointly perform computations on their respective private datasets without revealing sensitive information to each other.

The applications of differential privacy are diverse and extend beyond the examples mentioned above. As data privacy continues to be a critical concern in our increasingly connected world, differential privacy provides a principled and mathematically grounded approach to ensure privacy protection while enabling valuable data analysis and research.

Implementing differential privacy requires a careful balance between privacy guarantees and data utility. The choice of epsilon and the specific privacy mechanisms employed should be based on the sensitivity of the data, the context of the analysis, and the acceptable level of privacy risk. Adhering to best practices and guidelines in differential privacy is essential to ensure the effectiveness and reliability of privacy protection in data science applications.

Secure multiparty computation

Secure multiparty computation (MPC) is a field of study within cryptography and computer science that focuses on enabling privacy-preserving collaborative computations on sensitive data. It allows multiple parties to jointly perform computations on their private inputs while ensuring that no party learns anything beyond the final computation result. This section describes the concept of secure multi-party computing and its application in data science.

1. Introduction to Secure Multiparty Computation:

    Secure multiparty computation addresses the challenge of performing computations on data owned by multiple parties without revealing their individual inputs. Traditional approaches rely on a trusted third party to facilitate the computation, which poses a risk to privacy and introduces a single point of failure. Secure multiparty computation, on the other hand, enables the parties to perform the computation themselves while preserving privacy.

2. The Goal of Secure Multiparty Computation:

    The primary goal of secure multiparty computation is to enable collaborative computations while maintaining the privacy and confidentiality of the participants' inputs. The parties aim to compute a desired function on their combined inputs without revealing any sensitive information. The output should be the same as if the computation were performed on the combined inputs in a trusted, centralized manner.

3. Secure Multiparty Computation Techniques:

    Various techniques and cryptographic protocols have been developed to achieve secure multiparty computation. These techniques ensure that no party can gain information about the other parties' inputs during the computation. Some commonly used techniques include:

    a. Secure Function Evaluation (SFE): SFE protocols enable the parties to jointly compute a function on their inputs without revealing any intermediate values. The protocols utilize cryptographic techniques such as homomorphic encryption, oblivious transfer, and garbled circuits to securely evaluate the function.

    b. Secret Sharing: Secret sharing schemes divide the input data into shares and distribute them among the parties. The shares are designed in such a way that the original input can only be reconstructed when a sufficient number of shares are combined. This ensures that no party has access to the complete input data on its own.

    c. Zero-Knowledge Proofs: Zero-knowledge proofs allow a party to prove the correctness of a statement without revealing any additional information. These proofs are used in secure multiparty computation to validate the computations performed by the parties without revealing the inputs or intermediate values.

4. Applications of Secure Multiparty Computation in Data Science:

Secure multiparty computation has numerous applications in data science, enabling privacy-preserving collaborative analysis and computation. Some notable applications include:

   a. Privacy-Preserving Data Analysis: Data scientists can use secure multiparty computation to perform joint analysis on sensitive datasets without revealing the individual data points. This enables collaboration between different organizations or entities while preserving the privacy of the data.

   b. Collaborative Machine Learning: Secure multiparty computation allows multiple parties to train machine learning models on their private datasets without sharing the raw data. By jointly computing the model updates or aggregating the model parameters, parties can collaborate on building models without exposing their individual data.

   c. Secure Data Integration: Secure multiparty computation enables parties to integrate their data without sharing the raw data. By performing joint computations on encrypted or shared representations of the data, organizations can combine their data for analysis or decision-making purposes while preserving privacy.

    d.   Privacy-Preserving Statistics and Analytics: Secure multiparty computation can be used to compute statistics or perform analytics on combined datasets without revealing sensitive information. Parties can jointly compute aggregate statistics, correlations, or other analytical metrics without compromising the privacy of individual data points.

5. Challenges and Considerations:

While secure multiparty computation offers significant privacy benefits, there are challenges and considerations to be aware of:

    a.   Efficiency: Secure multiparty computation protocols can be computationally intensive, requiring significant computational resources and communication overhead. Optimizations and efficient protocol designs are necessary to make secure multiparty computation practical for real-world applications.

    b.   Trust Assumptions: Secure multiparty computation protocols often rely on cryptographic assumptions and the trustworthiness of the underlying cryptographic primitives. The security of the computation depends on the strength of these assumptions and the implementation of the protocols.

    c.   Scalability: Scaling secure multiparty computation to a large number of participants can be challenging due to increased communication complexity and potential performance bottlenecks. Efficient protocol designs and distributed computing techniques are necessary to handle scalability issues.

In conclusion, secure multiparty computation is a powerful technique that allows multiple parties to collaboratively compute on sensitive data while preserving privacy. Its applications in data science enable privacy-preserving data analysis, collaborative machine learning, secure data integration, and privacy-preserving statistics. While there are challenges to address, secure multiparty computation offers a promising solution for privacy-conscious data science applications.

Federated learning and homomorphic encryption

Federated learning and homomorphic encryption are two important techniques in the field of privacy-preserving machine learning. They enable data scientists to train models on distributed data without compromising the privacy of individual data points. In this section, we will explore federated learning and homomorphic encryption, discussing their principles, applications, and considerations.

1. Federated Learning:

Federated learning is a decentralized approach to machine learning where the training data remains on local devices or servers, and only model updates are exchanged between the central server and the participating clients. This paradigm allows for collaborative model training while keeping the data decentralized and reducing privacy risks.

2. Principles of Federated Learning:

The key principles of federated learning include:

    a.   Local Model Training: In federated learning, each client trains a local model using its own data. This local model captures insights and patterns specific to the client's data while avoiding the need to share raw data.

    b.   Model Aggregation: After local model training, the central server aggregates the model updates from multiple clients to create a global model. The aggregation process typically involves averaging the model parameters or using more advanced techniques such as Federated Averaging.

    c.   Privacy Preservation: Federated learning ensures privacy by keeping the training data on the client devices or servers. The central server only receives encrypted model updates and does not have access to individual data points.

3. Applications of Federated Learning:

Federated learning has numerous applications in scenarios where data privacy is crucial. Some notable applications include:

- a. Mobile Devices: Federated learning is particularly useful for training models on data collected from mobile devices, such as smartphones. By keeping the data on the devices and leveraging federated learning, user privacy is protected while enabling model improvements.

- b. Healthcare: In the healthcare domain, federated learning allows multiple hospitals or healthcare providers to collaboratively train models on patient data without sharing sensitive information. This enables better models for disease prediction, diagnosis, and treatment while maintaining patient privacy.

- c. Internet of Things (IoT): With the proliferation of IoT devices, federated learning provides a mechanism for training models directly on edge devices, reducing the need to transmit data to the cloud. This is beneficial for privacy-sensitive applications where data cannot leave the local network.

4. Homomorphic Encryption:

Homomorphic encryption is a cryptographic technique that allows computations to be performed on encrypted data without decrypting it. It enables data scientists to perform computations on encrypted data while preserving privacy.

5. Principles of Homomorphic Encryption:

The key principles of homomorphic encryption include:

    a. Encrypted Data: Homomorphic encryption allows data to be encrypted in such a way that computations can still be performed on the encrypted data without the need for decryption.

    b. Computation on Encrypted Data: Homomorphic encryption schemes support various mathematical operations such as addition and multiplication on encrypted data. These operations can be performed directly on the encrypted data without revealing the underlying plaintext.

    c. Result Decryption: After performing computations on encrypted data, the final result can be decrypted to obtain the output in its plaintext form.

6. Applications of Homomorphic Encryption:

Homomorphic encryption has several applications in privacy-preserving machine learning:

a. Secure Computation Outsourcing: Homomorphic encryption enables the outsourcing of computations to untrusted third-party servers while keeping the data encrypted. This is particularly useful when sensitive computations need to be performed in the cloud.

b. Private Machine Learning: By using homomorphic encryption, data scientists can train models on encrypted data without exposing the raw data to the training process. This allows for secure collaboration and model training while maintaining data privacy.

c. Secure Data Sharing and Collaboration: Homomorphic encryption facilitates secure data sharing and collaboration between multiple parties. Encrypted data can be shared with others, and computations can be performed on the encrypted data without the need to decrypt it.

In summary, federated learning and homomorphic encryption are powerful techniques for privacy-preserving machine learning. Federated learning enables collaborative model training on decentralized data, while homomorphic encryption allows computations to be performed on encrypted data without revealing the underlying information. These techniques have numerous applications in domains where data privacy is paramount, such as mobile devices, healthcare, and IoT. By leveraging federated learning and homomorphic encryption, data scientists can ensure privacy while still benefiting from the insights hidden in distributed and sensitive data.

Chapter Eight

Time Series Analysis in the Real World
Long Short-Term Memory (LSTM) networks for sequence modeling

Long Short-Term Memory (LSTM) networks are a type of recurrent neural network (RNN) that are specifically designed to handle sequential data and address the vanishing gradient problem typically associated with traditional RNNs. LSTMs have become a popular choice for various sequence modeling tasks, such as natural language processing, speech recognition, time series analysis, and more. In this section, we will delve into the concepts and workings of LSTM networks for sequence modeling.

1. Introduction to LSTM Networks:
   LSTM networks were introduced by Hochreiter and Schmidhuber in 1997 as an extension of traditional RNNs. The key advantage of LSTMs over RNNs is their ability to capture long-term dependencies in sequential data. They achieve this by introducing memory cells and gating mechanisms that allow them to selectively retain or forget information over time.

2. Structure and Components of LSTM Networks:
   LSTM networks consist of three main components: the input gate, the forget gate, and the output gate. These gates control the flow of information through the

memory cells, enabling LSTMs to effectively learn and retain important information over long sequences.

  a. Input Gate: The input gate determines how much new information should be stored in the memory cells. It takes input from the current time step and the previous hidden state and applies a sigmoid activation function to produce a gate value between 0 and 1. A gate value of 1 indicates full inclusion of the new information.

  b. Forget Gate: The forget gate controls the retention or forgetting of information in the memory cells. It takes input from the current time step and the previous hidden state and applies a sigmoid activation function. The gate value is multiplied element-wise with the existing cell state, allowing the LSTM to selectively forget irrelevant information.

  c. Output Gate: The output gate determines how much of the cell state should be exposed to the next time step. It takes input from the current time step and the previous hidden state, applies a sigmoid activation function, and passes the resulting gate value through a tanh activation function. The gate value is then multiplied element-wise with the updated cell state to produce the output.

3. Training and Backpropagation in LSTM Networks:

LSTM networks are trained using backpropagation through time (BPTT), which is an extension of the traditional backpropagation algorithm for recurrent neural networks. BPTT computes gradients by unrolling the LSTM network through time and propagating the error from the output to the input.

   a. Gradient Flow and Vanishing Gradient Problem: LSTMs address the vanishing gradient problem commonly encountered in traditional RNNs by utilizing gating mechanisms. The gates control the flow of gradients, allowing for more stable and efficient training of deep sequences.

   b. Long-Term Dependency and Memory: The design of LSTMs allows them to capture long-term dependencies in sequences. The memory cells store information over multiple time steps, allowing LSTMs to retain relevant information and mitigate the issues of vanishing gradients.

4. Code Example:

5.
```
import tensorflow as tf
from tensorflow.keras.layers import LSTM

# Define LSTM model
model = tf.keras.Sequential()
model.add(LSTM(128, input_shape=(timesteps, input_dim)))

# Compile and train the model
model.compile(optimizer='adam', loss='mse')
```

```
model.fit(x_train, y_train, epochs=10, batch_size=32)
```

This code sample uses TensorFlow to define an LSTM model for sequence modeling. An LSTM layer is added to the model, given the number of units (128 in this case) and an input form. The model is then compiled with an optimizer and loss function and trained on the training data.

LSTM networks enabled the capture of long-term dependencies in sequential data, revolutionizing the field of sequence modeling. It can retain relevant information over long sequences, making it particularly useful for tasks such as language translation, sentiment analysis, speech recognition, and time series prediction. By understanding the architecture and training process of LSTM networks, data scientists can harness their power to extract valuable insights from continuous data.

Multivariate time series analysis

Multivariate time series analysis is a field of data analysis that deals with datasets containing multiple variables observed over long periods of time. Analyze interdependencies, patterns, and dynamics between multiple time-varying variables to gain insights and make predictions. Multivariate time series analysis has applications in various fields including finance, economics, environmental sciences, healthcare, and more. This section reviews concepts and techniques used in multivariate time series analysis.

1. Overview of multivariate time series: A multivariate time series consists of two or more variables, each observed at multiple time points. For example, in finance, multivariate time series may include variables such as stock prices, trading volumes, and economic indicators. Analyzing such data requires understanding the relationships and interactions between these variables over time.

2. Visualizing time series data: Visualization of multivariate time series data is important for understanding patterns and relationships within datasets. You can visualize trends, correlations, and time dependencies between variables using techniques such as line plots, scatterplots, and heat maps.

3. Time series decomposition: Time series decomposition is a technique that decomposes a multivariate time series into its components: trends, seasonality, and residuals. This decomposition helps you understand the underlying patterns and extract relevant information from the data.

4. Granger causality analysis: Granger causality analysis is a statistical technique for determining causal relationships between variables in multivariate time series. Measures the predictability of one variable based on past values of another variable. Granger causality analysis helps identify leading indicators or predictors in multivariate time series.

5. Multivariate autoregressive model: Multivariable autoregression models, such as vector autoregression (VAR), capture dependencies and interactions among variables in multivariable time series. These models estimate the present value of each variable based on the past value of each variable and the past values of other variables in the system. VAR models provide a flexible framework for modeling and forecasting multivariate time series data.

6. State-space model: State-space models provide a powerful framework for modeling multivariate time series data. These models separate observed variables from underlying unobserved (latent) states. Kalman filtering and smoothing algorithms are commonly used to estimate latent states and make predictions. State-space models are especially useful when dealing with missing data, irregular sampling, and temporal time series.

7. Code Example:

```python
import numpy as np
import pandas as pd
import statsmodels.api as sm

# Load multivariate time series data
data = pd.read_csv('data.csv')

# Fit VAR model
model = sm.tsa.VAR(data)
results = model.fit()

# Forecast future values
forecast = results.forecast(data.values, steps=10)
```

```
# Print forecasted values
print(forecast)
```

In this sample code, we use the Statsmodels library in Python to fit a Vector Autoregression (VAR) model to a multivariate time series dataset. The data is loaded from the CSV file and the VAR model is initialized and matched to the data. We can then use the fitted model to predict future values by specifying the number of steps ahead. The predicted values are printed for later analysis.

Multivariate time series analysis provides valuable insight into the relationships and dynamics between many variables observed over time. By using appropriate techniques such as time series decomposition, Granger causal analysis, and multivariate autoregression, data scientists can uncover hidden patterns, make accurate predictions and make informed decisions in different areas dealing with time-changing data.

Forecasting with uncertain data and dynamic models

Forecasting using uncertain data and dynamic models is a complex task that occurs frequently in various fields such as finance, economics, supply chain management, and weather forecasting. Traditional forecasting techniques assume that historical data are accurate, stable, and free of uncertainty. However, in real-world situations, data can be subject to various sources of uncertainty, such as: B. Measurement errors, missing values, outliers, noise. Furthermore, patterns and relationships in data can change over time, necessitating the use of dynamic models that can capture these time-changing dynamics. Handling uncertain data:

When dealing with uncertain data in forecasting, it is important to incorporate probabilistic methods that can quantify and propagate uncertainty throughout the forecasting process. These methods help to express the uncertainty associated with future forecasts. One common approach is to take advantage of Bayesian inference, Monte Carlo simulation, and ensemble methods to account for uncertainty in predictive models. By using previous probability and distribution models, Bayesian forecasting provides a framework for combining uncertainty and generating probabilistic forecasts.

Dynamic model:

Dynamic models play an important role in forecasting when historical patterns change over time or exhibit non-linear dynamics. These models capture the variable nature of data over time and allow modeling of complex patterns and dependencies. By incorporating lagged variables, time-varying parameters, or state-space representations, dynamic models can more accurately capture trends, seasonality, and other time patterns. Examples of dynamic models include autoregressive integrated moving average (ARIMA), state space models, and dynamic regression models.

Parameters change over time:

In many forecasting situations, the relationships between variables or parameters in the forecasting model can change over time. Time-varying parametric models provide a solution by allowing parameters to be estimated at each time step, allowing forecasts to adapt to changing conditions. These models capture the dynamic nature of the data and make more accurate predictions than fixed parameter models.

Machine learning methods:

Machine learning techniques have gained considerable attention in forecasting due to their ability to handle dynamic and uncertain data. In particular, recurrent neural networks (RNNs) have shown great promise in capturing patterns and time dependencies in time series data. Short-Term Long-Term Memory Network (LSTM), a type of RNN, is good at capturing long-term dependencies and dynamic patterns. By leveraging deep learning models, it is possible to learn complex patterns and relationships from historical data and adapt forecasts to changing conditions.

Code Example:

```
import pandas as pd
from sklearn.model_selection import train_test_split
    from sklearn.ensemble import RandomForestRegressor

# Load uncertain time series data
data = pd.read_csv('data.csv')

# Split data into train and test sets
train_data, test_data = train_test_split(data,
test_size=0.2, shuffle=False)

# Prepare input and output variables
X_train = train_data.drop('target', axis=1)
y_train = train_data['target']
X_test = test_data.drop('target', axis=1)

# Train a random forest regressor model
model = RandomForestRegressor()
```

```
model.fit(X_train, y_train)

# Make predictions on test data
predictions = model.predict(X_test)

# Evaluate the forecast accuracy
accuracy = evaluate_forecast(predictions,
test_data['target'])

# Print the forecast accuracy
print(f"Forecast Accuracy: {accuracy}")
```

This code sample demonstrates a prediction approach using the random forest regressor model from Python's scikit-learn library. Uncertainty time series data is loaded, split into training and test sets, and prepared as input and output variables. A random forest regression model is trained on the training data and used to make predictions on the test data. Finally, the prediction accuracy is evaluated using the appropriate metric and the results are printed.

Forecasting with uncertain data and dynamic models requires specialized techniques to deal with the challenges posed by uncertain and time-varying data. Consolidating probabilistic strategies, energetic models, and machine learning approaches can make more precise expectations and account for the inalienable vulnerabilities in real-world information. These progressed estimating strategies empower choice creators to create educated decisions and viably arrange for long term.=====

Chapter Nine

Advanced Feature Engineering Techniques

Automated feature engineering

Automated feature engineering is a powerful technique in the field of data science that aims to automate the process of creating meaningful and informative features from raw data. Feature engineering plays a crucial role in machine learning and predictive modeling, as the quality and relevance of features heavily impact the performance and accuracy of models. Traditionally, feature engineering has been a manual and time-consuming task, requiring domain expertise and extensive experimentation. However, with the advent of automated feature engineering, this process can now be streamlined and accelerated using intelligent algorithms and techniques.

The goal of automated feature engineering is to discover and create new features that capture the underlying patterns and relationships in the data. It involves a combination of feature extraction, transformation, and selection methods that leverage statistical and computational techniques. By automating this process, data scientists can save time, reduce human bias, and explore a larger feature space more effectively.

Automated feature engineering techniques can be broadly categorized into two main approaches: traditional feature engineering methods and automated feature learning methods.

Traditional Feature Engineering:

Traditional feature engineering involves manually designing and creating features based on domain knowledge and intuition. It relies on human expertise to identify relevant variables, derive new features, and transform the data in a way that enhances the predictive power of the models. Some common techniques used in traditional feature engineering include:

Mathematical Transformations: Applying mathematical functions such as logarithm, square root, or exponentiation to the raw data to capture nonlinear relationships.

Interaction Terms: Creating new features by combining existing features through multiplication, division, or other mathematical operations.

Aggregation and Statistical Measures: Calculating summary statistics (mean, median, variance) or aggregating data over time periods (weekly, monthly) to capture trends and patterns.

One-Hot Encoding: Converting categorical variables into binary features to represent different categories.

While traditional feature engineering methods require manual effort, they offer the advantage of incorporating domain knowledge and providing interpretable features that can aid in model understanding and explainability.

Automated Feature Learning:

Automated feature learning methods, on the other hand, leverage machine learning algorithms and artificial intelligence techniques to automatically discover and create features directly from the data. These methods aim to learn feature representations that are optimized for the specific predictive task at hand. Some popular automated feature learning methods include:

1. Genetic Programming: Using evolutionary algorithms to iteratively evolve a population of mathematical expressions that encode features. The calculations explore for the finest combination of scientific operations and changes to maximize the model's execution.

2. Deep Feature Synthesis: Leveraging deep learning models, such as autoencoders or deep neural networks, to learn hierarchical representations of the data. These models automatically extract meaningful features from the raw input.

3. Feature Selection Algorithms: Employing algorithms that automatically select the most relevant features from a larger pool of candidates. These algorithms use statistical measures or machine learning models to

evaluate the importance and predictive power of each feature.

4. Feature Construction through Ensemble Methods: Combining multiple models or feature engineering techniques to create an ensemble of features. This approach can leverage the diversity and complementarity of different models to generate more robust and informative features.

Automated feature engineering techniques can be implemented using various programming languages and libraries. Python, with its rich ecosystem of data science libraries such as scikit-learn, featuretools, and TPOT, provides a wide range of tools for automated feature engineering.

Code Example:

```
import pandas as pd
from featuretools import dfs

# Load raw data
data = pd.read_csv('data.csv')

# Define entity and relationship
entityset = dfs.EntitySet(id='my_data')
entityset =
entityset.entity_from_dataframe(entity_id='my_table',
dataframe=data, index='id')

# Define target entity
target_entity = entityset['my_table']

# Generate new features using deep feature synthesis
features, feature_defs = dfs.dfs(entityset=entityset,
target_entity=target_entity, agg_primitives=['mean',
'max'], trans_primitives=['month', 'day'])
```

```
# Print the generated features
print(features.head())
```

In this example, we start by loading the raw data into a pandas DataFrame. Then, we create an entityset and define the entity and relationship within the dataset. Next, we specify the target entity for which we want to generate features. Finally, we use the dfs function from the Featuretools library to automatically create new features using deep feature synthesis. We can specify the aggregation and transformation primitives to apply during feature synthesis.

Automated feature engineering techniques offer significant benefits in terms of efficiency and effectiveness in generating informative features. By automating the process, data scientists can focus on model building and analysis rather than spending excessive time on manual feature engineering. These methods empower the investigation of a endless highlight space and can lead to progressed demonstrate execution and way better bits of knowledge from the information. In any case, it is imperative to note that computerized highlight designing ought to be utilized in conjunction with space information and cautious assessment to guarantee the produced highlights are important and adjusted with the issue at hand.

Feature selection and importance estimation

Include choice may be a basic step within the machine learning pipeline that points to recognize and select the foremost pertinent highlights from a given dataset. The objective is to decrease the dimensionality of the information by evacuating unessential or repetitive highlights, which can lead to made strides model performance, diminished overfitting, and improved interpretability. Highlight determination procedures help data researchers center on the foremost enlightening highlights and dispose of clamor or unessential data which will prevent the learning handle.

There are various feature selection methods available, ranging from statistical techniques to machine learning-based approaches. These methods can be broadly categorized into three main types: filter methods, wrapper methods, and embedded methods.

Filter Methods:

Filter methods are feature selection techniques that evaluate the relevance of features based on their intrinsic properties, such as statistical measures or correlation with the target variable, without considering the specific learning algorithm. These methods are computationally efficient and can be applied as a preprocessing step before model training. Some common filter methods include:

1. Correlation-based Feature Selection: Measures the linear relationship between each feature and the target variable using correlation coefficients, such as Pearson's correlation coefficient or Spearman's rank correlation coefficient. Features with high correlation are considered more relevant.

2. Mutual Information: Measures the amount of information shared between each feature and the target

variable. It captures both linear and non-linear relationships and is particularly useful for feature selection in classification tasks.

3. Chi-square Test: Applies a statistical test to determine the independence between each feature and the categorical target variable. It is commonly used for feature selection in classification tasks with categorical features.

Wrapper Methods:

Wrapper methods evaluate the performance of a learning algorithm using subsets of features and select the subset that maximizes the model's performance. These methods consider the specific learning algorithm and use it as a black box to evaluate feature subsets. They typically involve an iterative process that explores different combinations of features. Some popular wrapper methods include:

1. Recursive Feature Elimination (RFE): Begins with all features and progressively removes the least important features based on the model's performance. It repeatedly trains the model on a subset of features and eliminates the least significant ones until a desired number of features is reached.

2. Forward Selection: Starts with an empty set of features and iteratively adds the most relevant feature at each step based on the model's performance. It continues until a certain criterion is met, such as reaching a desired

number of features or achieving a specific level of performance.

3. Genetic Algorithms: Utilizes evolutionary algorithms to search for an optimal subset of features. It starts with a population of random feature subsets and applies genetic operators such as mutation and crossover to evolve the population and select the best feature subset.

Embedded Methods:

Embedded methods perform feature selection as part of the model training process. They incorporate feature selection within the learning algorithm itself, allowing the algorithm to optimize both feature selection and model performance simultaneously. Some popular embedded methods include:

1. Lasso (Least Absolute Shrinkage and Selection Operator): Applies regularization to the model's coefficients, encouraging sparsity and automatic feature selection. It can shrink some feature coefficients to zero, effectively eliminating them from the model.

2. Ridge Regression: Applies L2 regularization to the model's coefficients, which reduces the impact of less important features. Although ridge regression does not eliminate features entirely, it can help in reducing the impact of irrelevant or redundant features.

3. Random Forest Importance: Utilizes the importance measures derived from a random forest model to assess

the significance of each feature. Features with higher importance scores are considered more relevant and are given more weight in the model.

Code Example:

```
from sklearn.feature_selection import SelectKBest, chi2
from sklearn.ensemble import RandomForestClassifier

# Load the dataset
X, y = load_dataset()

# Apply Chi-square test for feature selection
selector = SelectKBest(score_func=chi2, k=10)
X_selected = selector.fit_transform(X, y)

# Train a random forest classifier on the selected features
clf = RandomForestClassifier()
clf.fit(X_selected, y)
```

This code example demonstrates how to use filtering techniques for feature selection, specifically the chi-square test. His SelectKBest class from scikit-learn is used with the chi2 score function to select k-top features based on their relevance to the target variable. Then train a random forest classifier on the selected features. This process allows us to focus on a reduced informative feature set, potentially improving model performance and interpretability.

Feature selection is a key step in the machine learning pipeline, helping to identify the most relevant features and discard irrelevant or redundant features. Different methods can be utilized for highlight choice, such as channel, wrapper, and inserting strategies. Choosing the correct strategy depends on the characteristics of your dataset, your specific learning calculation, and your desired result. By choosing the proper highlights, information researchers can make strides demonstrate execution, decrease overfitting, and pick up profitable experiences from their information.

Feature extraction by deep learning

Include extraction is an critical viewpoint of profound learning, leveraging pre-trained models to extricate valuable and significant representations from crude information. Profound learning models such as convolutional neural systems (CNN) and repetitive neural systems (RNN) are known for their capacity to naturally learn various leveled and theoretical highlights from information. By utilizing these pre-trained models, the learned representations can be utilized to extricate highlights that can be utilized for different downstream errands such as classification, question acknowledgment, and opinion examination.

The deep learning feature extraction process typically involves two main steps:

Pre-training and fine-tuning.

1. Pre-training:

    Pre-training refers to training a deep learning model on a large dataset. B. ImageNet for image-related tasks and text corpus for natural language processing tasks. During pre-training, the model learns to recognize and represent high-level patterns and features present in the data. This process involves iteratively updating the model weights using techniques such as backpropagation and gradient descent to minimize a specific loss function.

For example, for image-related tasks, CNNs can be pre-trained on large datasets containing millions of labeled images. As the network traverses layers, it learns to recognize edges, textures, shapes, and more complex visual patterns. Each level captures more abstract, higher-level properties. B. Part or Whole Object.

2. Fine-tuning:

Fine-tuning is adapting a pre-trained model to a specific task or area of interest. This step makes it possible to use the representations learned in the pre-training stage to extract features relevant to a particular problem. Fine-tuning typically involves freezing some layers of a pretrained model to save the learned representation, while modifying or adding new layers to adapt the model to the target task.

Code Example:

```
from tensorflow.keras.applications import VGG16
    from tensorflow.keras.preprocessing.image import load_img, img_to_array
from tensorflow.keras.applications.vgg16 import preprocess_input

# Load pre-trained VGG16 model
base_model = VGG16(weights='imagenet', include_top=False, input_shape=(224, 224, 3))

# Load and preprocess an image
image = load_img('image.jpg', target_size=(224, 224))
image = img_to_array(image)
image = preprocess_input(image)
```

```
# Extract features using the pre-trained model
features = base_model.predict(image.reshape(1, 224, 224, 3))

# Flatten the extracted features
features = features.flatten()

# Use the extracted features for downstream tasks
# ...
```

This code example demonstrates feature extraction using a pretrained VGG16 model. Loading a pretrained model using his VGG16 class from the Keras library and showing that we are interested in the extracted features rather than the classification, we exclude the top level (corresponding to the final classification level). increase. Next, load the image and preprocess using the appropriate preprocessing procedure for VGG16. Pass the preprocessed image to the base model to extract features. Finally, we reduce the extracted features to obtain a one-dimensional representation that can be used for further analysis and downstream tasks.

Feature extraction by deep learning has several advantages. First, you can leverage the power of pre-trained models trained on large datasets, saving significant computational resources and time. Second, these pre-trained models have already learned meaningful representations from the data that can capture important patterns and structures. This makes it very effective for feature extraction, especially in domains with limited labeled data. Finally, deep learning feature extraction offers a flexible and scalable approach that can be applied to different types of data such as images, text, and audio.

Deep learning feature extraction uses pre-trained models to extract useful representations from raw data. By using the learned features, you can improve the performance of downstream tasks and gain valuable insights from your data. Combining pre-training and fine-tuning, it can capture complex and abstract patterns, making deep learning a valuable tool for feature extraction in various domains.

Chapter Ten

Explainability and Interpretability in Machine Learning

Model interpretability techniques (LIME, SHAP)

Model interpretability is a crucial aspect of machine learning, especially when deploying models in real-world scenarios that require transparency and trust. Interpreting complex machine learning models helps us understand how they make predictions and provides insights into the factors driving those predictions. In this chapter, we will explore two popular model interpretability techniques: LIME (Local Interpretable Model-Agnostic Explanations) and SHAP (SHapley Additive exPlanations).

LIME is a model-agnostic technique that explains the predictions of any black-box model by locally approximating it with a simpler interpretable model. The key idea behind LIME is to create local explanations by perturbing the input data and observing the effect on the model's predictions. Let's illustrate the LIME technique with an example.

Consider a binary classification problem where we have trained a complex deep learning model to predict whether a customer will churn or not based on various features such as age, usage patterns, and customer history. Using LIME, we can generate local explanations for individual predictions. Let's say we have a particular prediction where the customer is classified as likely to churn. LIME will identify the most influential features for that prediction and provide a locally interpretable model that approximates the behavior of the black-box model in that neighborhood of the input data.

The strength of LIME lies in its ability to generate human-interpretable explanations, such as highlighting the importance of specific features in the prediction. This can be particularly valuable in domains where interpretability is critical, such as healthcare or finance. LIME has been widely used to interpret various machine learning models, including image classifiers, text classifiers, and recommendation systems.

Another powerful interpretability technique is SHAP, which provides a game-theoretic approach to explain the output of any machine learning model. SHAP values assign a numerical value to each feature, indicating its contribution to the prediction. SHAP values are based on the concept of Shapley values from cooperative game theory and provide a unified framework for feature importance estimation and interpretation.

SHAP values offer a global interpretation of a model by considering all possible feature combinations and their respective contributions. This enables us to understand the impact of individual features and their interactions on model predictions. SHAP values can be computed efficiently using different algorithms, such as TreeSHAP for tree-based models or KernelSHAP for kernel-based models.

Let's continue with our churn prediction example. Using SHAP, we can quantify the contribution of each feature to the likelihood of churn. For instance, we might find that customer age has a significant positive impact on the churn prediction, indicating that older customers are more likely to churn. Similarly, usage patterns and customer history may also have varying influences on the prediction. By visualizing the SHAP values, we can gain a comprehensive understanding of the model's decision-making process.

Both LIME and SHAP provide valuable insights into the inner workings of complex machine learning models. These techniques enable us to explain individual predictions or the overall behavior of the model, helping us build trust, detect biases, and identify potential issues. The generated explanations can be visualized in various ways, such as bar charts, heatmaps, or feature importance plots, making them accessible and understandable for stakeholders.

Implementing LIME and SHAP is relatively straightforward using available libraries and frameworks. For example, the lime library in Python provides a simple interface to apply LIME to any machine learning model, while the shap library offers tools for computing SHAP values and generating visualizations. Let's take a look at a code snippet demonstrating the application of LIME and SHAP:

```
# LIME example
import lime
import lime.lime_tabular

explainer =
lime.lime_tabular.LimeTabularExplainer(X_train,
```

```
feature_names=feature_names, class_names=class_names)
explanation = explainer.explain_instance(X_test[i],
model.predict_proba, num_features=5)

explanation.show_in_notebook()

# SHAP example
import shap

explainer = shap.Explainer(model)
shap_values = explainer(X_test)

shap.summary_plot(shap_values, X_test,
feature_names=feature_names)
```

By leveraging LIME and SHAP, data scientists can enhance the interpretability of their models and provide valuable insights to stakeholders. These techniques not only aid in understanding the decision-making process of complex models but also contribute to building transparent and trustworthy AI systems.

Rule-based models and decision trees

Rule-based models and decision trees are powerful and interpretable machine learning techniques that are widely used in various fields. These models provide a transparent and understandable framework for forecasting and decision-making, based on a predefined set of rules or hierarchy. This chapter introduces the concepts and applications of rule-based models and decision trees.

Rule-based models, also known as rule-based classifiers or expert systems, are built upon a collection of if-then rules. Each rule consists of a set of conditions (antecedents) and a corresponding action (consequent). The conditions are typically based on the values of input features, and the action represents the predicted class or outcome. These rules are manually crafted or learned from data using rule induction algorithms.

One of the most well-known algorithms for inducing rule-based models is the RIPPER (Repeated Incremental Pruning to Produce Error Reduction) algorithm. RIPPER combines rule learning with a pruning strategy to generate a set of accurate and compact rules. The algorithm starts with an empty rule set and iteratively adds rules that correctly classify instances while minimizing errors on unseen data.

Let's consider an illustration where we need to construct a rule-based show to foresee whether a client will churn or not based on their behavior and characteristics. We are able characterize a set of rules based on space information or by analyzing the information. For occurrence, a run the show may be:

"In case the customer's utilization is tall and they have been with the company for less than six months, at that point anticipate churn." By combining different such rules, we will make a comprehensive rule-based demonstrate.

Decision trees, on the other hand, are hierarchical structures that recursively split the input space based on feature values. Each internal node of the tree represents a feature test, and each leaf node represents a class label or outcome. Decision trees are constructed using various algorithms, with the most popular being the ID3 (Iterative Dichotomiser 3) and CART (Classification and Regression Trees) algorithms.

The construction of a decision tree involves selecting the most informative features to split the data at each node. The chosen features optimize a certain criterion, such as information gain or Gini impurity, to maximize the separation of classes or reduce the uncertainty. The tree is built recursively by partitioning the data based on the selected features until a stopping criterion is met, such as reaching a maximum depth or having a minimum number of instances at a node.

Decision trees are highly interpretable, as the path from the root to a leaf node represents a set of rules that collectively determine the prediction. Additionally, decision trees allow for feature importance estimation, as the importance of a feature can be inferred from the number of times it is used for splitting and the improvement it provides.

Let's illustrate the process of building a decision tree with a code example using the popular scikit-learn library in Python:

```
from sklearn.tree import DecisionTreeClassifier

# Create a decision tree classifier
clf = DecisionTreeClassifier()

# Train the classifier on the training data
clf.fit(X_train, y_train)

# Make predictions on the test data
predictions = clf.predict(X_test)
```

In this code snippet, we initialize a decision tree classifier and train it on the training data (X_train and y_train). The classifier learns the patterns in the data and creates a decision tree model. We can then use this model to make predictions on the test data (X_test) by calling the predict method.

Rule-based models and decision trees have numerous advantages. They are easy to interpret and provide transparent explanations for predictions. The rules or tree structure can be visualized, allowing stakeholders to understand the decision-making process. These models can handle both categorical and numerical features, and they are less prone to overfitting compared to more complex models.

However, rule-based models and decision trees also have limitations. They can struggle with capturing complex relationships in the data and may not generalize well to unseen data if the rules or splits are too specific. They can be sensitive to small changes in the data, which can lead to different rules or splits. Additionally, decision trees can become large and complex when dealing with high-dimensional data or datasets with many categorical features.

To mitigate these limitations, ensemble methods such as random forests and gradient boosting can be applied, which combine multiple decision trees to make more accurate predictions. These methods leverage the strengths of individual trees while addressing their weaknesses.

In summary, rule-based models and decision trees are valuable techniques in the data scientist's toolbox. They offer interpretability, transparency, and the ability to handle both categorical and numerical features. By understanding the concepts and applications of these models, data scientists can make informed decisions in various domains and effectively communicate their findings to stakeholders.

Model-agnostic interpretability methods

Model-independent interpretability techniques are powerful tools in the field of machine learning that provide insight into the inner workings of complex models without relying on specific architectures or assumptions. These methods provide a way to interpret and understand the decisions made by black-box models, allowing us to assess their fairness, reliability, and potential bias. In this chapter, we consider some common model-independent interpretability methods and their applications.

One widely used model-agnostic interpretability method is Local Interpretable Model-agnostic Explanations (LIME). LIME operates by approximating the local behavior of a complex model around a specific instance of interest. It works by sampling perturbations around the instance and generating a local, interpretable model to explain the predictions. LIME assigns weights to the perturbed instances based on their proximity to the instance of interest and fits an interpretable model, such as a linear regression or decision tree, to explain the model's behavior locally.

Let's illustrate the usage of LIME with a code example using the scikit-learn library in Python:

```
from lime import lime_tabular
    from sklearn.datasets import load_iris
    from sklearn.ensemble import import RandomForestClassifier

# Load the iris dataset
iris = load_iris()
X = iris.data
y = iris.target
feature_names = iris.feature_names
```

```python
# Train a random forest classifier
clf = RandomForestClassifier()
clf.fit(X, y)

# Create a LIME explainer
explainer = lime_tabular.LimeTabularExplainer(X,
feature_names=feature_names,
class_names=iris.target_names)

# Explain a specific instance
instance = X[0]
explanation = explainer.explain_instance(instance,
clf.predict_proba)

# Visualize the explanation
explanation.show_in_notebook()
```

In this code snippet, we first load the iris dataset and train a random forest classifier (clf) on the data. We then create a LIME explainer (explainer) using the LimeTabularExplainer class, specifying the feature names and class names. Next, we select a specific instance (instance) from the dataset and generate an explanation using the explain_instance method, which takes the instance and a prediction function (clf.predict_proba in this case) as inputs. Finally, we visualize the explanation using the show_in_notebook method.

Another popular model-agnostic interpretability method is SHAP (SHapley Additive exPlanations), which is based on cooperative game theory. SHAP assigns an importance value to each feature in a prediction by quantifying the contribution of each feature to the prediction outcome. It considers all possible coalitions of features and computes the expected contribution of each feature based on the Shapley value concept. The Shapley value ensures fairness and consistency in attributing the importance to each feature.

Let's demonstrate the use of SHAP with a code example using the XGBoost library in Python:

```python
import xgboost
import shap

# Train an XGBoost classifier
clf = xgboost.XGBClassifier()
clf.fit(X, y)

# Create a SHAP explainer
explainer = shap.Explainer(clf)

# Explain the predictions
shap_values = explainer.shap_values(X)

# Visualize the SHAP values
shap.summary_plot(shap_values, X,
feature_names=iris.feature_names)
```

In this code snippet, we train an XGBoost classifier (clf) on the iris dataset. We then create a SHAP explainer (explainer) using the Explainer class and compute the SHAP values for the dataset using the shap_values method. Finally, we visualize the SHAP values using the summary_plot function, which provides an overview of the feature importance.

Model-agnostic interpretability methods like LIME and SHAP offer valuable insights into the decision-making processes of black-box models. By using these methods, data scientists can explain individual predictions, identify important features, and assess the impact of different variables on model outcomes. These techniques contribute to model transparency, fairness, and trustworthiness, enabling stakeholders to make informed decisions based on the insights provided by these interpretability methods.

Chapter Eleven

Emerging Trends in Data Science
Edge computing and IoT analytics

Edge computing and IoT analytics are two interconnected concepts that play a vital part within the period of the Web of Things (IoT). As the number of associated gadgets proceeds to develop exponentially, conventional cloud-based approaches to information handling and examination confront challenges in terms of idleness, transmission capacity, and security. Edge computing offers a decentralized solution by bringing data processing and analytics closer to the edge devices, reducing the need for transmitting data to a remote cloud server. In this chapter, we will explore the key concepts and techniques involved in edge computing and IoT analytics.

At its center, edge computing includes the arrangement of computing assets, such as servers, capacity, and information handling capabilities, closer to the edge gadgets or sensors. This nearness empowers real-time or near-real-time information examination and decision-making, which is basic for time-sensitive applications. By preparing information locally at the edge, edge computing diminishes the idleness and transmission capacity prerequisites, making it well-suited for scenarios where moo idleness and tall transmission capacity are basic, such as independent vehicles, mechanical mechanization, and shrewd cities.

To demonstrate the concept of edge computing, let's consider a shrewd domestic situation. Envision a arrange of interconnected gadgets, counting sensors, cameras, and savvy machines, that produce a tremendous sum of information. Customarily, this information would be sent to a centralized cloud server for preparing and examination. However, with edge computing, the data processing and analytics tasks can be performed locally within the home itself. This localized approach reduces the response time for automated actions, enhances privacy by keeping sensitive data within the home network, and reduces the network traffic.

IoT analytics, on the other hand, centers on extricating significant experiences and information from the endless sum of information created by IoT gadgets. It includes the application of progressed analytics procedures to find designs, relationships, peculiarities, and patterns in IoT information. IoT analytics empowers businesses and organizations to form data-driven choices, optimize operations, and make strides client encounters.

Let's explore a code example that demonstrates IoT analytics using Python and the Pandas library:

```python
import pandas as pd

# Load IoT sensor data
df = pd.read_csv('iot_sensor_data.csv')

# Perform data cleaning and preprocessing
# ...

# Apply analytics techniques
# ...
```

```
# Generate insights and visualizations
# ...
```

In this code snippet, we start by loading the IoT sensor data from a CSV file using the Pandas library. We then perform data cleaning and preprocessing steps to handle missing values, normalize data, and handle outliers. Once the information is ready, able to apply different analytics methods such as expressive insights, time arrangement examination, machine learning calculations, or peculiarity location to extricate experiences from the information. At long last, able to produce visualizations, such as plots or dashboards, to communicate the discoveries viably.

Combining edge computing with IoT analytics opens up new possibilities for real-time data analysis, predictive maintenance, anomaly detection, and intelligent decision-making at the edge. By processing and analyzing data closer to the source, edge computing reduces the reliance on centralized cloud infrastructure, minimizes network latency, and enhances the overall system's scalability and responsiveness.

Furthermore, edge computing enables the implementation of advanced analytics algorithms directly on the edge devices themselves, leveraging their computational capabilities. This capability is particularly valuable in scenarios where immediate action is required based on the analyzed data, such as detecting anomalies in industrial machinery or triggering alerts for critical events.

In conclusion, edge computing and IoT analytics are integral components of the IoT ecosystem. By leveraging edge computing, organizations can perform real-time data processing and analytics closer to the edge devices, reducing latency, improving privacy, and enabling faster decision-making. IoT analytics techniques enable the extraction of valuable insights and knowledge from the vast amount of IoT data, enabling businesses to optimize processes, enhance operational efficiency, and deliver better experiences to customers. As the IoT continues to expand, the integration of edge computing and IoT analytics will become increasingly important in driving innovation and unlocking the full potential of IoT-enabled systems.

Quantum machine learning

Quantum Machine Learning (QML) speaks to the merging of two groundbreaking areas:

quantum computing and machine learning. It investigates the application of quantum computing standards and calculations to upgrade the capabilities of conventional machine learning models and address complex computational issues. In this chapter, we'll dive into the world of quantum machine learning, investigating its principal concepts, calculations, and potential applications.

Quantum computing, based on the standards of quantum mechanics, offers the potential to perform computations exponentially speedier than classical computers for certain issue spaces. It utilizes quantum bits, or qubits, which can exist in superposition states, permitting for parallel computation and complex information preparing. Qubits are the building squares of quantum machine learning calculations and empower the investigation of unused calculations that can use quantum impacts to fathom issues more effectively.

To understand the potential of quantum machine learning, let's examine a classical machine learning algorithm, such as a support vector machine (SVM), and how it can be enhanced using quantum computing principles.

```
from sklearn import svm
    from qiskit.aqua import QuantumInstance
    from qiskit.aqua.algorithms import QSVM

# Classical SVM
svm_clf = svm.SVC()
svm_clf.fit(X_train, y_train)
svm_predictions = svm_clf.predict(X_test)

# Quantum SVM
quantum_instance =
QuantumInstance(backend=qiskit_backend, shots=1024)
qsvm = QSVM(feature_map,
quantum_instance=quantum_instance)
qsvm.fit(X_train, y_train)
qsvm_predictions = qsvm.predict(X_test)
```

This code example compares a classical SVM classifier and a quantum SVM (QSVM) using the Qiskit library. A traditional SVM is trained on the training data (X_train and y_train) and used to make predictions on the test data (X_test). Quantum SVM, on the other hand, uses quantum feature maps and quantum instances for computation. Predictions made by the Quantum SVM are stored in qsvm_predictions.

Quantum machine learning has a few points of interest over conventional machine learning approaches. The most advantage is the potential of quantum calculations to productively illuminate certain computational issues. For example, quantum algorithms such as the Grover search algorithm and the quantum Fourier transform (QFT) can speed up data processing, optimization, and pattern recognition tasks.

These algorithms use inherent properties of quantum systems such as superposition and entanglement to explore large solution spaces more efficiently than classical algorithms.

Another promising area for quantum mechanical learning is large-scale data processing and analysis. Quantum computers can process huge data sets using quantum parallelism and quantum superposition. This capability has suggestions for assignments such as clustering, dimensionality decrease, and highlight determination, where conventional procedures battle to handle high-dimensional information.

In any case, it is critical to note that quantum machine learning is still in its earliest stages and faces critical challenges for commonsense application. A major challenge is the inborn affectability of quantum frameworks to commotion and decoherence. Quantum error correction techniques and improved qubit coherence times are essential to ensure the reliability and accuracy of quantum machine learning algorithms.

Additionally, quantum machine learning requires special hardware and expertise. Quantum computers are not yet widely deployed, and developing and optimizing quantum algorithms requires a deep understanding of quantum mechanics and quantum information theory.

Despite these challenges, the potential applications of quantum mechanical learning are enormous. Potential research areas include quantum-enhanced optimization, quantum neural networks, quantum clustering, and quantum generative models. Quantum machine learning also overlaps with other emerging technologies such as quantum chemistry, quantum physics simulation, and quantum cryptography.

In outline, quantum machine learning is an energizing wilderness within the field of machine learning, where quantum computing standards are combined with classical machine learning calculations to extend computational control. Quantum mechanical learning is still in its earliest stages, but it has awesome potential for understanding complex computational issues and extricating unused experiences from expansive datasets. Proceeded inquire about and advance in quantum computing equipment and calculations will shape long term of quantum machine learning and clear the way for groundbreaking applications in a assortment of areas.

Ethical considerations in emerging technologies

Moral contemplations in unused innovations are getting to be progressively critical as society gets to be more subordinate on progressed advances. The fast advancement and appropriation of advances such as fake insights, machine learning and mechanical technology raises numerous moral concerns that ought to be tended to in arrange to use these advances dependably and beneficially. This chapter surveys the most moral contemplations related with rising innovations and examines techniques for tending to them.

1. Fairness and Bias:

An important ethical consideration is ensuring fairness and reducing bias in new technologies. For example, machine learning algorithms can unintentionally perpetuate biases that exist in the training data. This can lead to discriminatory consequences in areas such as employment, lending and criminal justice. To address this issue, researchers and practitioners should employ techniques such as algorithmic fairness and bias detection to identify and mitigate biases in data and algorithmic decision making.

```
# Example of bias detection in machine learning
from aif360.datasets import AdultDataset
    from aif360.metrics import BinaryLabelDatasetMetric

dataset = AdultDataset()
privileged_group = {'race': 'Caucasian'}
unprivileged_group = {'race': 'African-American'}
metric = BinaryLabelDatasetMetric(dataset,
privileged_group, unprivileged_group)
disparate_impact = metric.disparate_impact()
```

In this code example, we use the AIF360 library to evaluate bias in a dataset. The AdultDataset represents a typical dataset used in tasks like employment screening, and we define privileged and unprivileged groups based on race. The BinaryLabelDatasetMetric calculates the disparate impact, which measures the difference in favorable outcomes between groups. By measuring inclination, we are able take remedial measures to guarantee reasonable decision-making.

1. Privacy and Data Protection:

The collection and investigation of tremendous sums of individual information in developing advances raise concerns around protection and information assurance. Techniques such as data anonymization, differential privacy, and secure data aggregation are employed to safeguard individuals' privacy while still enabling meaningful analysis. Privacy-preserving machine learning methods, including federated learning and homomorphic encryption, allow training models on distributed data without compromising individual data privacy.

```python
# Example of federated learning
import torch
import syft as sy

hook = sy.TorchHook(torch)
bob = sy.VirtualWorker(hook, id="bob")
alice = sy.VirtualWorker(hook, id="alice")

data = torch.tensor([[0.2, 0.6], [0.1, 0.5]])
target = torch.tensor([0, 1])

data_bob = data[0].send(bob)
target_bob = target[0].send(bob)

data_alice = data[1].send(alice)
target_alice = target[1].send(alice)

# Perform federated learning
model = torch.nn.Linear(2, 2)
optimizer = torch.optim.SGD(params=model.parameters(), lr=0.1)

for _ in range(10):
    optimizer.zero_grad()
    prediction_bob = model(data_bob)
    loss_bob = torch.nn.functional.cross_entropy(prediction_bob, target_bob)
    loss_bob.backward()
    optimizer.step()

    optimizer.zero_grad()
    prediction_alice = model(data_alice)
    loss_alice = torch.nn.functional.cross_entropy(prediction_alice, target_alice)
    loss_alice.backward()
    optimizer.step()
```

```
model.get().weight
```

This code example demonstrates the concept of federated learning, where data remains on individual devices (workers) while model updates are exchanged in a privacy-preserving manner. The data from Bob and Alice is not shared directly, ensuring data privacy while collectively training a model.

1. Transparency and Explainability:

Emerging technologies often operate as "black boxes," making it challenging to understand how they reach decisions. This lack of transparency raises concerns about accountability, trust, and the potential for biased or discriminatory outcomes. Techniques such as explainable AI, model interpretability methods like LIME and SHAP, and rule-based models provide insights into the decision-making process of complex models.

```
# Example of LIME for model interpretability
import lime
import lime.lime_tabular

explainer =
lime.lime_tabular.LimeTabularExplainer(data,
feature_names, class_names)
exp = explainer.explain_instance(data_instance,
model.predict_proba, num_features=5)

exp.show_in_notebook()
```

In this code example, we use the LIME library to explain the predictions of a machine learning model. LIME generates local explanations by perturbing input data instances and observing the corresponding changes in predictions. By highlighting the features that most influence the model's decision, we can gain insights into its behavior and assess its fairness, robustness, and potential biases.

2. Accountability and Governance:

Emerging technologies require robust governance frameworks to ensure accountability and responsible use. This incorporates characterizing clear rules, arrangements, and controls for the improvement and arrangement of these innovations. Moral survey sheets and multidisciplinary groups can give oversight and direction, advancing straightforwardness, reasonableness, and responsibility within the decision-making forms.

```
# Example of ethical review board evaluation
def evaluate_ethical_implications():
# Assess the potential ethical implications of the technology
pass

def propose_mitigations():
# Propose strategies to address ethical concerns
pass

def monitor_implementation:
    # Continuously monitor the deployment of the technology for ethical compliance
pass

# Ethical review process
evaluate_ethical_implications()
propose_mitigations()
monitor_implementation()
```

This code sample provides a simplified ethics review process for emerging technologies to assess ethical impact, suggest corrective actions, and monitor implementation to ensure continued ethical compliance. Such processes help us make responsible decisions and promote a culture of ethical considerations in technology development.

In rundown, moral contemplations play an critical part within the improvement and arrangement of modern innovations. By committing to reasonableness, security, transparency, accountability and administration, we are able guarantee that these innovations are utilized mindfully for the good thing about society as a entire. Following to moral standards and consolidating them into the plan and usage of modern innovations is basic to building believe, minimizing hurt, and maximizing the positive affect of these progresses.

Conclusion

In this book, we have secured a wide extend of progressed concepts within the field of information science and machine learning. As a recap, let's summarize a few of the key concepts talked about all through the book.

1. Neural Network Architectures:

We investigated different neural organize models such as Convolutional Neural Systems (CNNs), Repetitive Neural Systems (RNNs), and Generative Ill-disposed Systems (GANs). These architectures are widely used for tasks like image recognition, sequence modeling, and generating new data samples.

```
# Example of a CNN architecture
import tensorflow as tf
model = tf.keras.models.Sequential([
    tf.keras.layers.Conv2D(32, (3, 3), activation='relu', input_shape=(32, 32, 3)),
    tf.keras.layers.MaxPooling2D((2, 2)),
    tf.keras.layers.Flatten(),
    tf.keras.layers.Dense(10, activation='softmax')
])
```

2. Transfer Learning and Domain Adaptation:

Transfer learning enables the use of pre-trained models on one task to improve performance on another related task. Domain adaptation techniques address the challenge of applying models trained on one domain to another domain with different characteristics.

```python
# Example of transfer learning using pre-trained model
import tensorflow as tf
base_model = tf.keras.applications.MobileNetV2(input_shape=(224, 224, 3),
    include_top=False,
    weights='imagenet')
model = tf.keras.Sequential([
    base_model,
    tf.keras.layers.GlobalAveragePooling2D(),
    tf.keras.layers.Dense(10, activation='softmax')
])
```

3. Reinforcement Learning and Deep Q-Networks:

Reinforcement learning involves training agents to make sequential decisions through interactions with an environment. Deep Q-Networks (DQN) combine deep neural networks with Q-learning to enable agents to learn optimal policies in complex environments.

```python
# Example of Deep Q-Network (DQN)
import torch
import torch.nn as nn
import torch.optim as optim
import gym

class DQN(nn.Module):
    def __init__(self, input_size, output_size):
        super(DQN, self).__init__()
        self.fc = nn.Linear(input_size, 64)
        self.output = nn.Linear(64, output_size)

    def forward(self, x):
        x = torch.relu(self.fc(x))
        x = self.output(x)
        return x

env = gym.make('CartPole-v1')
model = DQN(env.observation_space.shape[0], env.action_space.n)
optimizer = optim.Adam(model.parameters(), lr=0.001)
```

4. Word Embeddings and Contextual Word Representations:

Word embeddings capture semantic relationships between words in a dense vector space, enabling better representation of textual data. Contextual word representations, such as BERT and GPT, leverage transformer models to capture context-dependent meanings of words.

```
# Example of using BERT for text classification
import transformers
import torch

tokenizer = transformers.BertTokenizer.from_pretrained('bert-base-uncased')
model = transformers.BertForSequenceClassification.from_pretrained('bert-base-uncased')

text = "This is an example sentence."
inputs = tokenizer(text, return_tensors='pt')
outputs = model(**inputs)
```

5. Graph Representation and Properties:
Graphs are powerful data structures for representing relationships between entities. We discussed various graph properties, such as centrality measures and community detection algorithms, which provide insights into the importance and groupings of nodes within a graph.

6. Bayesian Inference and Probabilistic Models:
Bayesian inference allows us to update our beliefs about unknown quantities based on prior knowledge and observed data. Probabilistic models, such as Bayesian Networks and Hidden Markov Models, enable reasoning

under uncertainty and modeling complex relationships between variables.

7. Markov Chain Monte Carlo (MCMC) Methods:
MCMC methods provide a way to sample from complex probability distributions. Techniques like Metropolis-Hastings and Gibbs sampling are commonly used for Bayesian inference and exploring high-dimensional spaces.

8. Probabilistic Programming Frameworks:
Probabilistic programming frameworks like Stan and PyMC3 provide high-level languages and libraries for specifying and performing Bayesian inference on probabilistic models. These frameworks simplify the process of building complex models and performing inference.

9. Policy Gradient Methods:
Policy gradient methods are reinforcement learning algorithms that directly optimize the policy of an agent. These methods use gradient ascent to update the policy parameters, enabling the agent to learn optimal policies in continuous action spaces.

10. Actor-Critic Algorithms:
Actor-Critic algorithms combine the benefits of value-based methods (like Q-learning) and policy-based methods (like policy gradients) by maintaining both a value function (critic) and a policy function (actor). This enables efficient learning of policies in reinforcement learning tasks.

11. Model-Based Reinforcement Learning:

Model-based reinforcement learning involves learning a model of the environment dynamics and using it to plan and make decisions. By using the learned model, agents can optimize their policies and achieve better performance.

12. Causal Inference Methods:
    Causal inference methods, such as propensity score matching and instrumental variables, help estimate causal effects and understand the causal relationships between variables in observational data.

13. Discovering Causal Relationships from Observational Data:
    Methods like graphical models and causal discovery algorithms enable the identification of causal relationships from observational data. These techniques aim to uncover underlying causal structures and infer cause-effect relationships.

14. Differential Privacy and Its Applications:
    Differential privacy provides a privacy guarantee by adding noise to data or query responses to protect individuals' sensitive information. It has applications in data analysis and machine learning, ensuring privacy while maintaining the utility of the data.

15. Secure Multiparty Computation:
    Secure multiparty computation enables multiple parties to jointly compute a function while preserving the privacy of their inputs. Techniques like homomorphic encryption and secure function evaluation enable secure collaboration without revealing private data.

16. Federated Learning and Homomorphic Encryption:
Federated learning allows training models across multiple decentralized devices without sharing raw data. Homomorphic encryption enables performing computations on encrypted data, preserving privacy during model training and inference.

17. Long Short-Term Memory (LSTM) Networks for Sequence Modeling:
LSTM networks are a type of recurrent neural network that can capture long-term dependencies in sequential data. They are widely used for tasks like language modeling, speech recognition, and time series prediction.

18. Multivariate Time Series Analysis:
Multivariate time series analysis involves modeling and analyzing data with multiple correlated time series. Techniques such as VAR models, state space models, and recurrent neural networks can capture complex dependencies in such data.

19. Forecasting with Uncertain Data and Dynamic Models:
Forecasting with uncertain data requires considering the uncertainty in data and modeling the dynamic nature of the underlying process. Techniques like Bayesian forecasting and state space models handle uncertain data and capture temporal dynamics.

20. Automated Feature Engineering:
Automated feature engineering techniques automate the process of generating meaningful features from raw data. Methods like feature selection, extraction, and

transformation help improve model performance and interpretability.

21. Feature Selection and Importance Estimation:
Feature selection techniques help identify the most relevant features for a predictive task, reducing dimensionality and improving model efficiency. Methods like recursive feature elimination and feature importance estimation aid in feature selection.

22. Feature Extraction with Deep Learning:
Deep learning models can learn meaningful representations from raw data using techniques like convolutional neural networks (CNNs) and autoencoders. These models extract high-level features automatically, enabling effective feature representation.

23. Model Interpretability Techniques:
Interpretability methods such as LIME (Local Interpretable Model-agnostic Explanations) and SHAP (SHapley Additive exPlanations) provide insights into how models make predictions. These techniques explain the contribution of features to model outputs.

24. Rule-Based Models and Decision Trees:
Rule-based models and decision trees provide transparent and interpretable models. They use a series of if-else conditions to make predictions, allowing easy understanding of the decision-making process.

25. Model-Agnostic Interpretability Methods:
Model-agnostic interpretability methods, such as feature importance, partial dependence plots, and permutation importance, can be applied to any machine learning model. These methods help understand the impact of features on model predictions.

26. Edge Computing and IoT Analytics:
    Edge computing involves performing data processing and analytics at the edge of the network, closer to data sources. This enables real-time decision-making, reduced latency, and efficient utilization of network resources in IoT (Internet of Things) applications.
27. Quantum Machine Learning:
    Quantum machine learning explores the intersection of quantum computing and machine learning. It investigates how quantum algorithms and quantum-inspired models can enhance machine learning tasks, such as optimization and pattern recognition.

28. Ethical Considerations in Emerging Technologies:
    As emerging technologies continue to advance, ethical considerations become crucial. This chapter investigates themes like predisposition, decency, straightforwardness, and responsibility within the advancement and sending of AI and machine learning frameworks.

In this book, we have secured a wide extend of progressed concepts in information science and machine learning. From neural systems and fortification learning to causal deduction and moral contemplations, these themes give a comprehensive understanding of the field's headways and challenges. By investigating these concepts, perusers can pick up the information and instruments to handle complex issues and make educated choices in real-world applications.

Dear readers,

Congratulations on completing "Data Scientist: Data Science in the Real World - Deep Dive into Advanced Topics and Emerging Trends." All through this book, we have taken you on a travel through the captivating world of information science, investigating progressed concepts, rising patterns, and the advancing scene of this energetic field. We trust this book has given you with important experiences, viable information, and a more profound understanding of the challenges and openings that information science presents.

As you reach the conclusion of this book, we energize you to reflect on your learning travel and consider the taking after key takeaways:

Persistent Learning: Information science may be a quickly advancing field, and remaining overhauled with the most recent headways is vital. Grasp a development attitude and commit to deep rooted learning. Investigate modern calculations, methods, and devices to grow your ability set and remain ahead of the bend.

Viable Application: The genuine esteem of information science lies in its viable application. Apply the concepts and methods secured in this book to real-world issues. Seek opportunities to work on diverse projects and explore different domains. By solving real challenges, you can make a tangible impact and drive innovation.

Ethical Considerations: Data science comes with ethical responsibilities. Be mindful of the potential biases, privacy concerns, and social implications of your work. Strive to develop responsible and fair models, considering the ethical implications at each step of the data science process.

Collaboration and Communication: Data science is a team sport. Collaborate with domain experts, stakeholders, and fellow data scientists to gain a comprehensive understanding of the problem and derive meaningful insights. Effective communication and teamwork are vital for successful data science projects.

Versatility and Adaptability: The field of information science is characterized by alter. Grasp the require for flexibility and adaptability as unused advances, apparatuses, and strategies develop. Be willing to investigate modern regions, try with distinctive approaches, and adjust to advancing industry patterns.

We trust this book has propelled you to seek after encourage investigation and experimentation in information science. Whether you're a prepared information researcher or a tenderfoot on this energizing journey, remember that there's continuously more to memorize and find. Grasp the challenges, look for out openings for development, and approach information science with interest, inventiveness, and a enthusiasm for problem-solving.

Thank you for joining us on this information science enterprise. We wish you continued victory in your information science endeavors and trust simply will make important commitments to the field. Keep investigating, improving, and changing the world with the control of information.

Happy data science journey!

Printed in Great Britain
by Amazon

35459045R00086